ANGRY
LIKE
JESUS

ANGRY LIKE JESUS

Using His Example to Spark Your Moral Courage

SARAH SUMNER

Fortress Press
Minneapolis

ANGRY LIKE JESUS
Using His Example to Spark Your Moral Courage

Cover design: Brad Norr
Book design: PerfecType, Nashville, TN

Library of Congress Cataloging-in-Publication Data is available
Print ISBN: 978-1-5064-0185-0
eBook ISBN: 978-1-5064-0186-7

The paper used in this publication meets the minimum requirements of American National Standard for Information Sciences — Permanence of Paper for Printed Library Materials, ANSI Z329.48-1984.

Manufactured in the U.S.A.

To *Ray Rood* and *Dallas Willard*

*If this book sparks a movement for moral courage
and moral leadership, then Ray Rood and the late Dallas Willard
are the godfathers of this movement.*

Their sage advice has helped steer the course of my life.

Contents

Acknowledgments

How do I thank the people who have supported me in the long, extended project of birthing this book? First, I thank the chair of my dissertation committee, the late H. O. J. Brown, my Harvard-bred professor who treated me more like a colleague than a student. Second, I want to thank Wayne Grudem, who was the first professor to champion my research on godly anger—which explains why I selected him to be the second reader in my doctoral committee. Third, I thank Nigel Cameron and Douglas Moo, who each served as the director of the PhD program at Trinity Evangelical Divinity School when I was there. I wouldn't be "Dr. Sumner" without the signatures of these four men.

Since I wouldn't be "Sarah" at all without my parents, I want to thank them as well. My father got me started in grade school as a young theologian. Not only did he instill in me a positive fear of God, he also modeled what it means to repent. I wrote an essay about my father's fantastic ending—his extremely inspiring last hour—which can be accessed in the blog section of my website, www.rightonmission.org /blog. My mother tirelessly served us kids and read Bible stories to us when we were little. I had just the right parents to shape me, so I could grow up to write this book.

Thanks also to Becky and John, my sister and brother, who applauded my work early on, and for my sister-in-law, Cindy Quek

Chambers, who invested time reading the manuscript after I produced the first draft. I appreciate Cindy's eagerness to serve. She is such a giving sister and friend.

My husband's sister, Debbie Draper, read the book early as well and encouraged me richly. Debbie's assurances are salve to my soul. Debbie can articulate the nuances of pain in a way that makes her seem like the most understanding person in the world. Debbie and her husband, Ron Draper, are both dear to me.

I thank all my friends who have prayed, including Rachel Pilli, Shelly Gibbs, Barb Takahashi, Becky Durben, Frank Strazzarino, Rick Caldwell, Brad Allen, my precious godchildren, Jacob and Eliana Aguilar, and my extra special friend, Maxine Collord, who has walked with God longer than perhaps anyone else I know. Maxine is in her nineties. Every week or two, she and I write each other letters through the regular mail. No one in my life has ever spoken to me the way Maxine does. Her words to me sound like heaven. Maxine has read the manuscript twice so far, and she's praying for all the readers of this book.

Thanks also to the Friday-morning women at Willow Creek Community Church, who were the very first recipients of my teachings on godly anger back in the early 1990s. When I was a doctoral student, I used to go to school—load up my wagon, so to speak—and pull my load of scholarly learning over to Willow, where these beloved women, all hundred fifty of them, would lap it up. I hope they recall that I formally dedicated my dissertation on godly anger to them. Thanks also to the men in the men's ministry that I started at Willow Creek. They, too, heard my research on godly anger. Being a teacher and, really, a pastor to these women and men was one of the greatest joys of my life. Their questions and affirmations fed into my thinking and played into the formation of this book.

One particular attendee in the men's class in those days expressed more excitement than the rest did. That man would be Jim Sumner, who is now my husband. Thank you, Jim, for championing this book with so much zest and zeal. Thanks also for being supportive of my countless hours of writing, for proofreading the final draft, and for listening to me read to you out loud. Most of all, I thank you for your love. But thanks also for all the silly songs you sing. Of all your many styles, I still like your Willy Nelson and operatic voices best, and always I adore it when you hum.

Next, I want to thank Susie Kimes. Little did I know when I gazed from afar with deep appreciation for the founder of Chosen Women that Susie would become my close friend. During a very harsh season of my life, Susie took me to see Jesus in Revelation 1:17. She said to me, "This is the Jesus that God wants you to see." She showed me the risen Lord whose eyes shine like the sun in all its strength. She read to me how John, the apostle, fell down like a dead man before Jesus. Then she pointed out that Jesus put his hand on John. I realized then and there that God, with perfect timing, had prompted Susie Kimes to assure me, undoubtedly, that God had my back. Jesus' hand has been on my back throughout my rawhide journey. Lord willing, in due time I will share the spiritual drama of my recent testimony, the one I didn't mention in this book.

Thanks, too, to all my friends who wrote endorsements. I could say something special about each of them. Extra thanks to Judy Klaustermeyer and all the Young Life women at Lost Canyon, including Sue Micetic and Angie Gillette, who cheered as I cast a vision for a "movement for moral courage" fueled by godly anger that ushers in God's love. Judy, in particular, has ministered encouragement to me.

Unique thanks to Martha Stinton, Academic Dean at New Hope Christian College in Honolulu, for coming up with the title of this book and for being such a generous friend. Special thanks also go to Pastor Jim Domen, who expands my national network. Jim's go-power and enthusiasm are a boon for the marketing of this book. Thanks also to Melissa Brosch, who read an early draft and cheered; and to Pastor

Bill Feeser, who praised the book and supported me as my pastor in this project.

I also extend thanks to Dr. Halee Gray Scott, my former student and colleague, whom I hired when I was dean of A.W. Tozer Theological Seminary. Halee stands out because she is brave and soulful. Her commitment to Jesus is encapsulated in the title of her book, *Dare Mighty Things*. Halee is a writer whom I expect to ferment like fine wine.

With regard to the development of *Angry Like Jesus*, I thank Andrea Buczynski, whose gift of wisdom has been blessing me for years. Her feedback on this book was insightful. Something similar needs to be said about the unmatched help I received from Sherman Williams, who combed through every line in 2013 and again in 2014, long before the editors at the publisher ever saw it. I'm pretty sure I implemented every single change Sherman suggested. Sherman's careful eye and high standards of ministry excellence have helped me to achieve my goals. Special thanks as well to J. I. Packer, who also read two different iterations of the full manuscript, which I overhauled again after that. When he told me on the phone, "Sarah, your book has a tremendous punch to it!" I felt triumphant.

Thanks, of course, to Fortress Press, particularly Tony Jones, who latched on to my book proposal very quickly; Lisa Gruenisen, who did a nice job of flagging spots in the manuscript that needed to be adjusted in order to respect a larger audience; Marissa Wold Uhrina, who internally managed the project of bringing the book to print; and Karen Schenkenfelder, who very competently and graciously prodded me to be accurate in every jot and tittle in this book. I am grateful for them all, and I am thrilled with Tony's idea for the subtitle.

Finally, I thank my two closest work companions. I'll begin with Leigh Williams, who jump-started me by telling me her dream job is to help promote my vision and all that it entails. Leigh is a spark plug. She volunteered to do everything she can to extend the reach of *Angry Like*

Jesus. I think she has read it twice now, if not three times already. Leigh ministers to me so much that I call her "Pastor Leigh," and after she speaks, I often say, "The prophetess has spoken." Leigh's hugs and heart and fortitude help set the standard at Right On Mission.

Last, but not least, there is Pakou. Pakou Vang is my right-hand person. She is so enormously helpful that I can hardly begin to explain it. She came up with the title for chapter 4. She contributed hundreds and hundreds of hours to building our website, including the web page for *Angry Like Jesus.* She draws out content from me. She produces marketing materials for this book. She intercepts and intervenes and saves me from making mistakes. I am so thankful for her giftedness and willingness to compensate for my weaknesses. Pakou could win the forbearance award. She is very detail oriented and exceptionally considerate and reliable. Furthermore, she is as supportive on an emotional level as she is administratively. She's so pleasant that I tell her she has "sparkle dust."

In my experience, Leigh and Pakou are the two most responsive listeners on the planet. Their diligence and radiance shine and outshine the dark troubles we have seen. There's nothing I'd like more than to work with them until I finish my course (Acts 20:24).

Foreword

Our world is not as it should be. We all have moments when we find the world to be different than we imagined it would be. Sometimes these moments of discovery are mere shadows flitting past us on an otherwise sunny day when we hear of misfortune that is distant and remote. Other times, these moments roar in like a tsunami, as when death, divorce, sexual assault, a random act of violence, or a medical diagnosis turns our sunny lives into a nightmare.

How do we bear up under the weight of such profound disappointment? How do we face loss? How do we answer the horror of inexplicable evil?

This book is a compass that helps us find our way out of confusion, and Sarah Sumner a reliable guide to show us how to navigate difficult terrain until we reach a place of beauty that we didn't know was there before.

I first met Sarah as a graduate student at Azusa Pacific University. I went to study theology because I wanted to know more about the God I love, but also because I wanted to understand the deep injustices I experienced from the hands of church leaders. As a young girl, I watched my pastor's marriage fall apart because of an extramarital affair. When I was a teenager, my church community shunned me and my brother because of our parents' divorce. When I was a college student, a youth pastor raped me. I wanted to understand the spiritual failures of these leaders, so that I could learn how to teach leaders to have integrity and honor.

When I entered seminary, I was a gutted girl, hollowed out by trauma. But my professor, Dr. Sumner, taught me to consider the overlooked limits of evil. Evil is indeed evil (there's no sense in denying or minimizing it), yet God providentially overcomes evil with good. In Sarah's book, we see this brilliantly in Jesus. Every story of Jesus turns evil on its head and proves again that love is stronger than death.

As my mentor, Sarah Sumner helped me grapple with my own failings. We all have ways of filling those empty places left by injustice. Some people silently slide into the comfortable pseudo-safety of slothful ease. Some brim with eruptive rage. Some, in resignation, turn to the Numbing Things (e.g., alcohol, drugs, fast-track sex, false religion, big money, overachievement). I chose to protect myself with flinty indifference. As happened to Sarah, my parents' divorce led me to an eating disorder that consumed more than a decade of my life. My life, back then, did not overflow with the soft, strong love of God, because I would not admit my anger. Sarah's wisdom gave me confidence, validated my grief, and offered me very needed space to be angry.

In this book, Dr. Sumner will help you, too. What you have here in your hands is strong medicine that is sweet, not bitter. Godly anger does demand that we lay down our vain excuses and accusations, yet it also gives us power to dare mighty things and triumph in ways we never thought possible. One of my favorite lines is when Sarah speaks of "the reality that some things can't be done for the sake of the kingdom apart from the gift of Jesus' anger."

A Hasidic rabbi once taught this simple prayer: "Let me not die while I am still alive." The stories about Jesus in this book reach deep into the places long devastated and shine light on wounds we have long misunderstood and tried to run from. When Jesus swoops in, the demons flee. Hear the good news: Jesus' anger ushers in God's upside-down kingdom that turns the world right side up.

Halee Gray Scott
Littleton, CO
June 4, 2015

HOPE
has two beautiful daughters;
their names are anger and courage—

ANGER
at the way things are
and
COURAGE
to see that they do not remain
as they are.

—Author unknown

Chapter 1

Introducing Jesus' Anger

Anger has a place in the Christian life. Not the political kind of anger that produces "angry Christians." Not the nasty kind of anger that gets smeared around when protesters write hate mail. Not malice. Not acrimony. Not irrational, worldly anger.

The world is brimming over with the *wrong kind* of anger. So much ugly anger is pumped into family feuds, divorces, fallouts between friends, trolling, road rage, unresolved disputes, incivility in fights, church splits, religious claims, cutthroat competitions, violent crimes, and all-out war.

But ugly anger is not what Jesus had. Jesus had a different kind of anger. Given the actual history of humanity's sins of anger, it's understandable why some Christians are reluctant to believe the world might need a dose of Jesus' anger.

Jesus wasn't a sinner; he was perfect. Yet most people have overlooked the example of perfect anger Jesus gives us. What if Jesus' anger is for our good? Have you ever heard a sermon about imitating Jesus' good anger?

Can you think of any praise song about Jesus' perfect anger? Have you ever asked God to help you to be angry like Jesus?

Christians believe that people need Christ's love. Isn't Jesus' anger part of Jesus' love? Wasn't Jesus showing love for his Father when he drove out the money changers who made God's house of prayer a den of robbers (John 2:13-22)? I bet Peter felt loved after Jesus rebuked him, saying, "Get behind me, Satan!" (Matthew 16:23), because six days later, Jesus took Peter with him to witness Jesus' transfiguration (Matthew 17:1-5). I myself feel loved on account of Jesus' anger. Jesus' anger healed me. It airlifted me out of a pit that I fell into. Thus, I cannot begin to thank God enough for acquainting me with the anger Jesus had.

Welcome to This Book

This book is about the anger of real love. It's a book that shows the beauty of angry love. It's a book that tells how angry love refuses to lower God's holy standards of protectiveness. Jesus wants to protect us from awful things that happen when people are too unyielding to trust God. Jesus' anger elbows us, reminding us of the truth that God is faithful.

If everyone trusted God, godly anger would be superfluous—unnecessary. Jesus' anger is needed on account of people's doubts in the integrity of the God whom Jesus trusted. We do not trust God as Jesus did. That's why we have anger that is sinful, and that's why we instead need anger that is godly. I'll explain that more, especially in chapters 3 and 9.

For now, I shall explain how this book is laid out. To begin with, I have conformed it to the policies of Fortress Press. That means, by default, that I quote from the New Revised Standard Version of the Bible (NRSV) unless I make it plain that I am quoting instead from the New American Standard Bible (NASB) or from another Bible translation. It also means I use no footnotes, which will probably invite more readers. After all, this line of books is called "Theology for the People." In addition, it also means there are no study questions included in this book. I do, however, provide a study guide with questions about *Angry Like Jesus* for those who join my blog, which is connected to my website at www.rightonmission.org.

The structure of the book is straightforward. Chapter 1 introduces the concept of Jesus' anger. Jesus' anger shows us what godly anger is. Chapter 2 describes how sinful anger differs from godly anger. Chapter 3 deepens the conversation by exploring how godly anger relates to grief and pain. Chapter 4 reveals the source of godly anger and describes God's wrath in hell. Chapters 5–7 display my own imagination as I recount stories that illustrate the beauty of Jesus' anger. Chapter 8 explains why Jesus' famous cry of dereliction on the cross, "My God, my God, why have you forsaken me?" (Mark 15:34), was *not* a cry of anger. It was the greatest cry of faith in all of history. Chapter 9 details the tragedy of what happens when people fail to have godly anger. Chapter 10 casts a vision of the transformative effect of Christlike anger that salts the earth.

Jesus' anger salts the earth. Without the salt of Jesus' anger, people accept what's unacceptable. We allow what we shouldn't allow. We don't make changes we should make. We deceive ourselves into thinking that corruption doesn't need to be opposed. We leave it to God. We stay hands-off. Conveniently, we take ourselves off the hook. When we lack Jesus' anger, we allow evil to prevail.

I realize that it's strong language to use the word *evil*. But evil is real. Sometimes evil comes in the form of ISIS beheadings or a holocaust. More often, it occurs as greed or selfish fear. Greed hardens people by draining them of empathy and leaving them to unsavory devices. Selfish fear does the same. Selfish fear and greed are subtle evils. Part of what makes them evil is they pretend *not* to be evil. But both are deeply lodged in human pride.

Turning away from pride requires humility. The English word *humility* derives from the Latin word *humus*, which means "earth."

As Christians, we're commanded to be earthy—like salt. Salt is so down-to-earth that it refuses to cave in to the fallen human tendency to deny truth rather than face it. Salted anger is not afraid. It assumes responsibility. It motivates us to confront things we wish did not exist.

Salt is gritty. It's an irritant, yet medicinal. Jesus' anger was medicinal. It was irritating and gritty precisely because it was salted by truth. Salted anger makes people well enough—spiritually healthy enough—to stop denying truth. The salt of righteous anger is needed in this world because the world is a dangerous place. *Deliver us from evil,* we pray. The salt of Jesus' anger is God's gift to help deliver us.

"You are the salt of the earth," Jesus said. "But if the salt has become tasteless, how will it be made salty again?" (Matthew 5:13, NASB). People who aren't salted become cynical. Cynicism breeds hopelessness—"Why try to make things better when they're not going to get better?" Cynicism is anger in disguise. It pulls down people's perspectives with bad memories of frustration and been-there-done-that-it-didn't-work fatigue. Cynicism turns people into quitters.

Professor Henri Nouwen used to say that cynicism is "cold anger." The thrust of what I'm saying is that cynical anger weighs people down. Jesus' anger, by contrast, lifts people up and gives them hope. Jesus' anger hopes against all hope. When Jesus died on the cross, he spurned the work of the devil *in hope* that none might perish, but that all might come to repentance on account of his loving sacrifice of himself. To put it in the grammar of my own creative language, Jesus' anger wasn't cynicized. It was salted.

Salt preserves the truth of the difference between right and wrong. Salted people remember that right is better than wrong. Salted individuals have truth in their inmost parts. Jesus said, "I am the truth" (John 14:6). As followers of truth, we have a calling to tell the truth, not only to each other, but to ourselves.

When Jesus said to his disciples, "You are the salt of the earth," I believe he was saying that those who fear the Lord are the *conscience* of the earth. If we aren't salty salt, we have no flavor. We hold back. Salt is only salty when it's truthful. When Christians ignore the truth, society misses out. There's no irritant—no salt—to help heal society's wounds unless Christians are openly honest about the truth.

Seared consciences in the church promote seared consciences in society. For example, the seared consciences of priests who were convicted for crimes of child abuse gave way to *more* seared consciences that enabled pederasty in the football locker room at Penn State. Tragically, in both cases, there was no accountability until the lawyers and the courts became involved. Where were the bishops? Where was the Penn State board?

Governance today, even in Christian organizations, is typically so broken that expensive external force is the only thing potent enough to prompt internal change for the better. What's happening in the mainstream culture is happening in the church subculture. Accountability is becoming a joke; thus, integrity is becoming a joke. Hope is now becoming a joke as well.

Now that America is said to be "post-Christian," Americans are becoming post-hope. This book is meant for Christians who are struggling to have hope. I wrote this book especially for agitated people who refuse to be post-hope but who need help in figuring out how to be strong. There is so much hopelessness in Christian churches and organizations. I believe this hopelessness is grounded in bad theology, particularly with regard to our wrong theological thinking about anger.

The Need for Jesus' Anger

As a Christian girl in Texas, sheltered as I was, I never knew about godly anger until after my Christian parents were divorced. Their divorce shook like an earthquake in me. Here I was, "Sweet Sarah," who never got mad. That's what my mother called me—Sweet Sarah. But now I was twenty-two, and my parents had just split up, and I could not feel anything but the aftershock.

Despite my privileged upbringing, I was ill equipped to face the breakdown of my beloved family unit. I wasn't mature enough to transcend the disequilibrium of disturbances within myself caused by my anxiety and grief. So I started losing weight. And the skinnier I became, the more I felt in control of the pain deep in my soul that I denied.

My denial was not deliberate. I was not aware of my own pain. I knew I didn't feel good, but it didn't occur to me that I might be angry. My preoccupation was that I couldn't find Sweet Sarah. I couldn't settle down or find my normal self or my normal family.

I knew I was upset, yet it was hard for me to access the truth of my negative feelings, because I wanted to be a good Christian. I didn't know that Christians could be angry in a truly Christian way. Due to the unbiblical theology I grew up with, I didn't think it was right for a genuine Christ follower to be angry. I thought anger, by definition, was sinful. My impression from weekly church lessons was that holiness prohibited human anger. As far as I was concerned, it was my inner consternation (not anger!) that troubled me. My inner consternation seized my sense of self and threatened my Christianity. You see, I couldn't afford to be honest about my unacceptable anger, because I myself did not approve of it.

I did not want to be angry.

How many people are disregarding God precisely because they're censuring their own anger? How many are revolting because they're trying to be happy, yet life is making it hard for them to cope? How many well-churched people are secretly embittered against God? How many feel incapable of loving the living God who has allowed them to be visited by evil? How many professing Christians are conflicted inside, waging war against themselves, because they're failing to be honest about their anger?

Many of us know what it is to be disillusioned. Dis-illusioned. To diss an illusion. To be awakened by the thought that things are different from how they seemed. To dismiss a view of life that isn't real. Practically every person is painfully disillusioned at some point. Therefore, we have protested and cried about the outrageousness and absurdity and hideousness of evil. Yet I would venture to say that we've done this without realizing God *wants* us to be angry, but not in the usual way that we might think. God wants us to be angry in a different kind of way, with a different kind of anger. That's what this book is about—different anger. Jesus' anger. What I call "salt."

Salt is salty. It isn't bitter or sour or sweet. It isn't mean (as bitterness and sourness are), and it isn't nice (as churchy sweetness pretends to be). Salt is powerful enough to heal a giant wound or melt a glacier. Yet too much salt is ruinous, not only to the taste of food, but also to the health of a human body. Excessive salt causes high blood pressure. Too much anger does the same.

But a healthy amount of the right kind of anger turns the church into a self-cleaning oven. It pulls pastors out of depression and congregants out of complacency. It awakens Christian board members and elders. It brings victims out of victimhood. It defies the gravitas of self-pity. Glimmering godly anger rouses Christians to get up. It spotlights our big sins, so we can see them. It shows us that our problem is that we aren't trusting God.

Godly Anger and Forgiveness

The salt of godly anger partners with forgiveness. Consider Pope John Paul, who went to visit his would-be assassin, Mehmet Ali Agca, in prison. The pope went to express his forgiveness. What the pope did *not* do was ask for the prisoner's release. The pope's forgiveness did not make discipline unnecessary. Nor did the pope's forgiveness dismiss the need for justice and ongoing civil protection for society.

Yes, forgiveness is the hallmark of Christianity. To forgive is to let go of hateful anger. To forgive is to set bitterness aside. The pope forgave Mehmet Ali Agca, but he did not excuse him or say that attempting murder is acceptable.

To trivialize the problem of irresponsible behavior is to enable. Dysfunctional enablement puts up with chronic unrepentant sin. Enablement lets people keep being destructive. The enabling wife of an alcoholic husband, for instance, tolerates and perpetuates his drunkenness. Godly anger, by contrast, does not. Coupled with forgiveness, godly anger says, "I forgive you, yet I respect you enough to hold you to account, even though I'm not here to punish you."

Pope John Paul didn't punish Agca. The government confined Agca in his prison cell in congruence with God's plan for legitimate power to mitigate evil (Romans 13:4). The pope, I believe, forgave Agca and then put any latent anger aside.

Scripture says all anger—regardless of whether it's sinful or godly—is daily to be set aside. Paul says, "Do not let the sun go down on your anger" (Ephesians 4:26). Every night, we as Christians are commanded to take a vacation away from anger. I don't mean that literally, in a crude, simplistic way, as if to say a person can't be angry in the middle of the night when someone is raped. The point is that godly anger takes rest. It regularly rests. If it is fighting a long-term battle against a behemoth, godly anger may pick up again in the morning, but as soon as evening comes, it rests again.

All old anger is sinful. Only fresh anger can be godly. Anger is like manna. Overnight it rots. It turns rancid in a matter of hours. In other words, every kind of anger is perishable. Another way to say it is that sinful anger is acid, and godly anger is soap. Acid and soap both burn skin. Thus, both need to be rinsed off. Forgiveness is a rinse. It washes off all anger, removing the burn of acid *and* soap.

Three Disclosures

Since anger is so potent, it's important to be cautious as we proceed into the rest of this book. For this reason, I intend to be extra careful in the way I speak about it. Thus I would like to offer three disclosures.

First Disclosure

Writing a book on Jesus' anger daunts me. The last thing I want to do is spur people to indulge in self-approved resentment in the name of Jesus Christ. Resentment never has a rightful place. Resentment is essentially fleshly. Fleshly anger forgets that vengeance belongs to God. It's the *law* that does the avenging here on earth. The apostle Paul explains that "the law" is a "minister of God, an avenger that brings wrath on the one who practices evil" (Romans 13:4, NASB). God has given us recourse through the laws we have on earth, so that we can stand for truth without indulging in sinful anger, even if it seems needful to file a lawsuit.

The other thing this book is *not* meant to promote is petty church splits over doctrinal disagreements. Since I am a theologian, I understand the importance of right doctrine, yet I also know that Scripture says to teach "with great patience and instruction" (2 Timothy 4:2, NASB). So let me try to establish that godly anger isn't meant for attacking people, especially other believers who are honestly seeking truth but coming up with different spiritual insights. Jesus' anger never blasted against the Sadducees, for example, for saying that there is no resurrection.

Second Disclosure

All of us are inclined to see our own anger as godly when it's not. Chances are our anger isn't godly. There is wisdom in the statement made by a friend of mine: "Whatever can be done *with* anger can be done better without it." But there is also something missing from that claim: an acknowledgment of the reality that some things can't be done for the sake of the kingdom of God apart from the gift of Jesus' anger.

Consider David, who killed Goliath, and Queen Esther, who saved her people. In both Old Testament stories, godly anger produced great courage in each hero. When Goliath taunted God, the mighty men of Israel ran away. David alone chose to face the giant. Because David had faith in God, he also had moral courage that came to him in the form of godly anger. David said to Goliath:

> You come to me with a sword, a spear, and a javelin, but I come to you in the name of the LORD of hosts, the God of the armies of Israel, whom you have taunted. This day the LORD will deliver you up into my hands, and I will strike you down and remove your head from you. And I will give the dead bodies of the army of the Philistines this day to the birds of the sky and the wild beasts of the earth, that all the earth may know that there is a God in Israel. (1 Samuel 17:45-46, NASB).

Similarly, when Haman plotted genocide for the Jews, Esther had the singular courage to take action against Haman's wicked schemes. Aside from Mordecai, Esther's Jewish cousin, the rest of the Jewish people collectively fell into group panic when Haman arranged for an edict to be pronounced against the Jewish population. It was Esther, no one else, who decided to approach the Persian king. Queen Esther knew full well that simply standing before the king unsolicited was a violation of Persian law unless the king decided to extend his favor. How did Esther summon the courage to blow the whistle? I believe she did so by abhorring the evil that Haman had devised. Esther's abhorrence of evil made her angry with the right kind of anger.

It was socially risky for Queen Esther to take on Haman. Haman was so adept in his political maneuvering that Haman did not seem evil to most people. Similarly, David took a risk at a relational family level by taking the initiative to size up Goliath's strength. Goliath was so impressive that when David peered down to see what the giant looked like on the battlefield, David's brothers put down David, not Goliath.

It took so much moral courage for David and Queen Esther to stand up for what is right. Both confronted foes who had good résumés. Both took on opponents who were respectable in society. Both opposed leaders of notoriety.

David and Esther risked their very lives. Their anger was self-giving, not self-indulgent. David didn't have to fight Goliath. Esther wasn't forced to take on Haman. Both went out of their way to challenge evil.

Because David and Esther chose to take decisive, angry action, two colossal evil agendas that were targeted against God—and therefore targeted against God's people—were both thwarted. After David killed Goliath, the Philistine army was slain. After Esther exposed Haman, Haman's plan for the annihilation of the entire Jewish people was abruptly turned on its head such that Haman was hung on the gallows he had spitefully prepared for Esther's cousin.

All that is to say that Jesus' kind of anger is powerfully beneficial. It can even save a whole nation.

This is not to say, however, that anger is always needed. Often it's *not* needed. When Jesus called the multitudes—sinners—to follow him, never did he preach to them in anger. Jesus' anger is not a weapon to be used against sinners in society. Jesus is a friend of sinners. He's an advocate for those who need to hear his loving call and realize that his love can make them clean. Jesus welcomes sinners to come home. It's when people deny the fact that we ourselves are sinners that our dishonesty provokes the ire of God.

Third Disclosure

I have been re-salted in the process of producing this long gestated book. Believe it or not, this book has been in the making for over twenty-five years. Slowly it emerged from my study of the Scriptures, my scholarly theological endeavors, and also the real footprints of my faith. I wrote it from my heart, not just my head.

To offer a glimpse of the backstory, when I was in my twenties, I started studying godly anger independently in the context of my quest to live for Christ. What drove me to this subject were my questions about anger that I didn't know how to process theologically in the wake of my parents' divorce. I selected the topic of godly human anger for the sake of my own spiritual formation. As the basis of my study, I read the Bible twice from cover to cover and asked God to help me see what godly anger is, if there were even such a thing at all. After I shared my initial findings with my seminary professors, they affirmed me to the point of allowing me to write a biblical theology of godly human anger as the subject of my doctoral dissertation.

Unrelated to my research, but as part of my pursuit of purposeful living, I crafted a mission statement for myself: "to build integrity in the church." For me, doing this was not a rote exercise. All this time, my life mission statement has been encoded inside my life trajectory. For over two decades now, I have consciously been trying to build integrity in the church and to live out what I have learned about godly anger.

When at one point a prominent publishing company offered a generous contract for me to write a book on godly anger, I couldn't bring myself to sign the paper. Now I understand that I simply wasn't ready to write this book. Back then, I had not yet fused my mission statement (to build integrity in the church) with my doctoral research (on godly anger) to give me the perspective I have now. Although both concepts guided my thinking, they were two discrete ideas in my mind. It wasn't until I walked through some unexpected losses that I cognitively reached convergence. Suddenly, everything came together in my efforts to write this book, once it finally dawned on me that godly anger is a mechanism for building integrity in the church.

So here I am today with the final revised version of these pages. The long, extended process of writing and rewriting has been humbling yet restorative for me. Visiting and revisiting Jesus' pain and Jesus' anger has helped me understand Jesus' faith. Jesus' faith was honest. He truly trusted God. Because Jesus trusted God, Jesus wasn't characteristically angry. When Jesus *did* get angry, his faith kept his anger clean and pure. Jesus' faithful anger magnificently triumphed over evil.

I can't help but wonder how empowered we could be to overcome evil ourselves, as Christians, if we would trust in God as Jesus did. Jesus *trusted* God because he *knew* God. He knew God because he *obeyed* God. He obeyed God because he *loved* God. Unless we honestly love God, we won't really care about obeying God. Unless we obey God, we won't know God. If we don't know God, we won't trust God.

When Christians don't trust God, we become fearful and insecure—too fearful to stand up for what is right. Fear makes people less truthful. Fearful people are too weak to carry truth. When we Christians become so fearful that we refuse to imitate Jesus, we may gain the world, but it will be at the expense of losing our capacity to trust God.

Godly Anger and Integrity in the Church

Hebrews 11:6 unequivocally states that without faith, it is "impossible" to please God. Part of having faith is trusting God to forgive our sins, but another part of faith is trusting God to the point that we *stop doing* our sins. Daring to act rightly is the way to build integrity in the church.

But now, who am I—a sinner—to attempt to build integrity in the church? Answer: I am someone willing. I'm available to God for this. I am a partaker of God's grace. I'm someone Jesus died for. No one has to be perfect in order to be used by God to make things better. If we surrender ourselves to God and admit the humbling truth of who we are and what we've done, God will do something marvelous with that. I believe our repentance makes us game changers. It changes the game, so to speak, when one is truthful enough to admit one's personal shortcomings and work toward correcting them.

How can we correct our own shortcomings? I, for one, can't do so without other people's help. So years ago, in my twenties, I started praying a crazy prayer: *Lord, help me to love correction—to just* love *it!* I believe that that prayer has really helped me. I have made great progress because I have been so helped by other people.

Which would you rather be: uncorrected and stuck, or corrected and delivered from your sin? I would rather be healed, wouldn't you? I am still asking God to help me love correction, even though it's rare for most professing Christians (especially positional leaders) to trust each other enough to offer and receive gifts of correction.

It's impossible for any of us to be a faithful friend unless we love each other enough to disrupt each other's worst sin patterns. I imagine we agree that to stage an intervention for a self-destructive addict is a loving thing to do, not a caustic thing to do. Sure, the addict might feel judged. During an intervention, the addict *is* judged. It takes good judgment to discern that a person is an addict who needs help. This principle applies in all relationships; it takes good judgment to become a faithful friend.

Godly anger makes us faithful friends. Proverbs 27:6 says, "Faithful are the wounds of a friend" (NASB). A faithful friend is true enough to "wound" another person with truthful confrontations when that person is unrepentant yet professing to be a follower of Christ. "Care-frontation" is a gift from a faithful friend. It's when Christians *don't* confront—when we fail to care enough to help each other repent and be restored and get on mission and stay on track—that we miss out.

Virtually every Christian I know claims to want to experience more of God's presence. Yet how quickly we forget that turning away from evil—repenting from our sin—invites the palpable presence of the Lord. We each move closer to God when we repent. If we draw near to God, God draws near to us (James 4:8). Repentance makes it possible for us to experience God in fresh new ways.

Some time ago, I was asked to speak to a group of about a hundred high school kids who were connected to the police department in Los Angeles. These kids all hailed from homes that were unstable and unsafe. I was told before addressing them that some of the kids slept on mattresses that were laid directly on the floor, not placed on bed frames, because their beds needed to be lower than the bedroom window, since at any given time, a bullet might fly through that window. These kids were well acquainted with corruption. They had seen authority figures, including their own parents, abuse power. These kids were not naive. After teaching them for two hours or so about what it means to have good character, and after apologizing to them on behalf of all the adults who had betrayed them, I asked them if they thought they could have better character themselves. I said something like "Raise your hand if you know you haven't tried that hard to be humble, courageous, and honest in the way you live your life. Raise your hand if you know you could do better—I'm not talking about being perfect, I'm just asking if you know you could do better starting today."

Every person in the room raised a hand.

Of course, none of us are able to stop making mistakes. To some extent, all people are going to be somewhat sinful. We simply have to bear each other's fallenness. But God gives common grace. By the power of God's grace distributed commonly to all, we can practice basic decency together. We won't be perfected until our Lord returns, but in the meantime, we can grow. We can blossom into people we never dreamed we'd be. We can be freed from subtle fears that limit us in our ethical development. We can remove our masks. We can choose to be truthful. We can be salt.

A Note of Assurance

Generally speaking, this book is more informative than instructive. It teaches rather than trains. I have chosen this approach because people are set free, not by a list of do's and don'ts, but by hearing the basic principles of reality. "The truth will make you free," said Jesus (John 8:32). Commandments do not make people free. If you were simply told to stop being bitter or stop doubting God, you probably would not be able to stop. But if someone were to convince you that God is on your side, and that you have no need to fight and clamor desperately for yourself, then your rancor might subside. It's the knowledge of the truth—the truth of God's great love—that miraculously sets people free. Jesus said, "And you shall *know* the Truth, and the Truth shall make you free" (John 8:32, NASB, italics added).

The truth is God is for us, not against us (Romans 8:31). Do you know that? Or have you merely been informed without believing it quite yet? I believe that the more you know this truth, the less you will feel compelled to resort to sinful anger in self-defense. Eternal God is for us, together and individually. The more we understand that, the more we can trust God in the day of evil. Infinite God is *for* me. Infinite God is *for* you. The more we truly believe that, the more able we become to step out in godly anger to make things right.

Jesus' anger makes things right. It's part of his spiritual legacy to us. I wrote this book specifically to recipients of Jesus' legacy. I wrote it for the purpose of helping people understand that while sinful anger extinguishes love, godly anger ignites it.

Chapter 2

Doesn't the Bible Say Anger Is Sinful?

Many churchgoing Christians are simply unaware of what godly anger is. No one ever told them that in the four Gospel accounts in the New Testament, Jesus showed godly anger no less than fifteen times. People like me were taught that anger is inherently sinful. Others were told that anger is one of the "seven deadly sins." It's true that most anger is deadly, but godly anger is vibrant and enlivening. According to the Scriptures, godliness requires us to be angry at certain times. It's a biblical imperative: "Be angry, and yet do not sin" (Ephesians 4:26, NASB).

The apostle Paul says that our "new self" is to "be angry." I marvel at the fact that in all my years of church going and formal Bible training, never was I told this. Yet Scripture says it plainly. First, it says to put on the "new self" (Ephesians 4:24, NASB), and second, to "speak the truth" (4:25), and third, to "be angry, and yet do not sin" (4:26). We are to be angry with anger that is truthful, even about the condition of our own heart. Godly anger is truthful. It doesn't exaggerate or distort things to favor human pride. Truthful anger is humble enough to be honest. Paul implies that it takes a "new self" to be angry without sinning, because the new self is "created according to the likeness of God in true righteousness and holiness" (4:24).

Other parts of Scripture, however, teach us *not* to be angry. Two verses in particular are often cited as prohibitions against anger of every kind. First, there is James 1:20 (NASB), "The anger of man does not achieve the righteousness of God," and second, there is Matthew 5:22 (NASB), "Whoever is angry . . . is guilty." In light of Jesus' anger, what are we to make of these verses? Let's examine them as found in the New American Standard Bible (NASB).

James 1:19-20

At first glance, James 1:19-20 completely closes the case for righteous anger: "This you know, my beloved brethren. But let everyone be quick to hear, slow to speak, and slow to anger; for the anger of man does not achieve the righteousness of God." James is unequivocal. He speaks to everyone. James says that "everyone" should be "slow to anger." His reason, he says, is that the anger "of man" does not achieve the righteousness of God.

"For the anger of man," he says. The anger of *andros*. The Greek word *andros* refers either generically to people or specifically to males. So the question needs to be asked: Is James saying that male anger—as opposed to female anger—is sinful? To my knowledge, no scholar in church history has ever argued so. Common sense tells us that James is referring to human anger in general.

But what exactly does James mean? Is he saying that anger is sinful precisely because it is human? Given that Jesus was fully human and that Jesus had sinless anger, we can logically deduce that humanness itself does not make anger sinful. In other words, anger is not defiled by pure humanity. Since Jesus, who was 100 percent human, had godly anger, it's conceivable that you and I can have godly anger, too. I believe Jesus' anger proves that human anger can be good.

Let's think a little more about what human anger is. Human anger is human, not divine. Whereas God's divine anger transcends all human motives and desires, human anger, by contrast, is grounded in fallen motives and desires. The word *fallen* here refers to what theologians call the "fall," the first sin of Adam and Eve. When Adam and Eve sinned, the whole creation fell. (To understand how their sin marred all of creation, think of how one smashed fly stirred into the soup ruins the whole pot of soup).

Fallenness accounts for everyone's propensity to sin. Fallen anger is what we have when we are grumpy because we're hungry or exhausted. Fallen anger is loveless. The angry fits of two-year-olds who stomp to get their way are fits of fallenness that give way to actual sin. It's empirically verifiable that no one has to be taught how to generate sinful anger.

Animal anger, by contrast, is not sinful. Though some animals are rogue, that is not the same as being sinful. Animals are fallen, not sinful. To be fallen is to be marred with imperfection. Many animals observably express fallen anger. Bears growl, cats hiss, and dogs bite. Yet animals don't have malice. That's why animals don't hold grudges. Animals don't have anger tied to egotistical pride.

Charles Darwin wrote a book on the emotions of animals. His observations and conclusions have been extremely influential. Darwin's view of animal anger—that it is totally instinctive—has been applied to human beings by most clinical professionals, including Christian psychologists and atheist Sigmund Freud. In Freudian circles, anger is understood to be biological. Thus it has been said that Freud regards anger as "a nearly uncontrollable animal passion."

Looking back again to the New Testament book of James, I don't think James was saying that the "anger of *andros*," the anger of "man," cannot achieve the righteousness of God because human anger amounts to "uncontrollable animal passion." If that were the case, then James would have refrained from telling people to be "slow" to anger, since people would not be able to control their uncontrollable primal passion. To assert that human emotions are primarily biological—and not volitional and moral as well—is to promote a Freudian ethic of nonresponsibility.

Therefore, I believe "the anger of man" in the book of James specifically refers to the anger of sinful flesh (the anger of *andros*). James means to be saying that sinful anger cannot achieve the righteousness of God.

Now consider what James does *not* say. He does not say, "Never be angry." Nor does he say that anger itself is sinful. James says to "be slow" to anger. Being told to be slow to do something is very different from being told not to do it at all. Nowhere in the Bible are we told to be slow to commit adultery or be slow to lie. In other words, James does *not* tell us to be slow to sin. The implication then is this: just as we are to speak—and yet be "slow to speak," so we are to be angry with the right kind of anger—yet, even then, be "slow to anger."

Matthew 5:22

What about Jesus' words in the Sermon on the Mount? "But I say to you that whoever is angry with his brother shall be guilty before the court" (Matthew 5:22, NASB). According to church tradition, many Christians have believed that Jesus forbids his followers to be angry. It's been said by commentators that Matthew 5:22 is an absolute prohibition of all anger. Since even pagans of the past, such as Cicero, have openly denounced the folly of human anger, many thinkers have asserted that people know intuitively that anger is always wrong.

Is it true that all anger is folly? No, it is not. There is also a long tradition both inside and outside the church that says anger can be virtuous at times. Countless commentators have understood Jesus' claim in Matthew 5:22 not as a blanket statement against all anger, but rather as a clarifying statement to point out the spiritual fact that senseless violence, such as murder, stems from sinful anger in the heart.

God judges the human feelings behind human actions. Anger that leads to murder is offensive in God's sight. So Jesus denounces anger, not just murder. That is not to say, however, that Jesus changed the Sixth Commandment, "You shall not murder" (Exodus 20:13) into a stricter commandment, "You shall not be angry." What Jesus categorically condemns is the vilifying anger of murder. "Whoever is angry" with murderous anger shall be "guilty," *whether or not that anger is ever acted out.* It is the anger behind the murder that renders guilt.

The word for anger that Matthew uses here is *orge* (pronounced ore´ gay). *Orge* is anger that can be either sinful or godly. In Ephesians 4:31, the apostle Paul says that *orge* should be "put away." This *orge* is simmering anger—sinful anger. We can see this sinful anger fleshed out in the famous parable of the prodigal son in Luke 15:11-32 when the *orge* of the elder brother simmered against his father and prodigal brother. However, *orge* is godly anger in the story where Jesus had *orge* at the Pharisees who were watching to see if Jesus would heal a man on the Sabbath (Mark 3:5). *Orge here* is the anger Paul affirmed. "Be angry (*orgizesthe*), and yet do not sin," Paul said (Ephesians 4:26, NASB).

So you see, there is godly *orge* and sinful *orge*. I therefore conclude that in Matthew 5:22, Jesus prohibits sinful *orge* that may or may not explode into senseless violence but that festers in the form of unforgiveness.

What Is Anger?

It's important to pause to define what anger is. A book on godly anger doesn't mean much if all I have done is redefine the word *anger* so that it points to something other than real anger. So let's back up and verify the fact that godly anger truly is a kind of anger.

Biblical Greek has no word for godly anger. If it did, it would be easier for people to see the distinction between anger that is godly and anger that is sinful. It's also unfortunate that the English language has no word for positive, good anger that is righteous. I guess someone could attempt to innovate a new word such as "sangry" (a combination of the words *salt* and *angry*) or "gdangry" (a combination of the words *good* and *angry*). I defer to readers to decide for themselves if these types of verbal contrivances are worth keeping. Meantime, I won't use them. I'll just stick with classic language.

Because people don't all agree on what anger is, it's important to discuss the definition. What is anger? Here are a few contemporary dictionary definitions of it:

- "A strong feeling of displeasure and usually of antagonism" (Merriam-Webster.com)
- "A feeling of great annoyance or antagonism as the result of some real or supposed grievance" (Collins English Dictionary)
- "The strong feeling you get when you think someone has treated you badly or unfairly, that makes you want to hurt them or shout at them" (Macmillan Dictionary)

According to these dictionary definitions, anger is a feeling. A strong feeling. A strong feeling of displeasure or annoyance. Anger happens as a result of being burdened with a real or perceived grievance, and it makes you want to hurt whomever you perceive has harmed you.

The English word *anger* derives from the Old Norse word *angr*, meaning "grief," which in turn comes from the Latin word *angh*, meaning "tight, constricted, or painful," as from the Latin verb *angere*, which means "to strangle or draw tight." In Greek, the word is *ankein*, which means "to squeeze" or "to embrace" and bears the more related form, *ankhone*, which connotes the idea of strangling. The Germanic root is similar, yielding the familiar word *Angst*. Other related words in English include *anguish, anxiety, agony, agonism,* and *antagonism.*

Anger is complex because it's always tied to something underneath. Anger is not a prime number, so to speak. There is always something more basic under anger, such as envy or guilt or embarrassment or fear or wounded pride or jealous love. That's why anger is broadly known as a secondary emotion, not a primary emotion.

Though it's way too big a task to take full inventory of the nuanced definitions of anger that have been used over the centuries, it's helpful to consider a few contemporary definitions. A medical expert might say, for instance, that anger is a corrosive emotion that can run off with your mental and physical health. Or that anger is a healthy emotion that is perfectly normal. A psychologist might say that anger is usually a healthy emotion that helps you protect your own best interests. Or, conversely, that anger can lead to problems when it comes from an unhealthy place in your inner psyche.

A number of psychologists, including Christian psychologists, have contended that anger itself is neutral. I strongly disagree with that claim. Anger is *not* neutral. Granted, a knife is neutral. A knife is an instrument that can be used either for ill by a murderer or for good by a surgeon. A knife is a tangible object that is "out there." Anger, by contrast, is "in there," in a person. Anger is *part of* a person. Anger is embodied within a person who has motives and desires. Human anger therefore is charged by human wants and motivations. It is positively charged by what a person *does* want and negatively charged by what a person does *not* want. What we want and don't want drives our anger. We, as people, don't feel angry unless there's something we want or don't want. If we don't really care one way or the other, we will not feel angry. So you see, there's really no such thing as neutral anger.

It has medically been shown that a number of physical ailments, such as heart problems, digestive problems, headaches, skin flare-ups, and sleep disorders, can be symptoms of festering anger. Mental illnesses, too, such as depression and anxiety disorders, often stem from unaddressed anger. That's why counselors and psychologists work so hard to assist people in identifying their anger, so it can be consciously processed before it tacitly gives way to crime, mental illness, self-destructive behavior, or any other kind of harmful action.

Two Ancient Views of Anger

As we continue to consider what anger is, let's look back very briefly into ancient history at two famous philosophers, Seneca and Aristotle. Though neither were Christians themselves, both were so widely respected that their views on human anger influenced early theologians in the church. Indirectly, both Aristotle and Seneca have shaped Christians' ideas on anger to this day. To increase our understanding of the big picture, let's begin with a brief review of Seneca.

Seneca

Seneca (4 BC–AD 65) was a Roman, an adviser to the emperor Nero, and a promoter of Stoicism. Stoicism is a philosophy that was founded by a man named Zeno in the fourth century BC. Stoics reject emotions altogether. They especially reject anger. To be stoic means to be unemotional, impassive, and impervious to pain.

Whereas Aristotle said in his *Nicomachean Ethics* that "anger listens somewhat to reason," Seneca said in his essay *De Ira*, "If anger listens to reason and follows where reason leads, it is no longer anger, of which the chief characteristic is willfulness." Seneca believed that anger, by definition, is irrational and unruly. In Seneca's view, anger is "not anger" unless it is "useless."

Seneca also said that a person's mind collapses whenever it is moved by passion. He said anger "overleaps the reason and sweeps it away." Seneca further said, "The other vices may incite the mind; anger overthrows it." Seneca thus concluded, "Anger, I say, has this great fault—it refuses to be ruled." Anger, according to Seneca, is "ungovernable." Thus Seneca insisted that no one should suppose that "at any time, in any place, it [anger] will be profitable." He said, "Let us not try to regulate our anger, but be rid of it altogether—for what regulation can there be of any evil thing?"

Was Seneca right? Is anger actually useless? Did God give human beings the capacity to be angry for no purpose? What do you think? Did Jesus prohibit anger completely? Or are some Christians reading Seneca into Jesus?

Fourth-century theologian Gregory of Nyssa is one of those in church history who disagreed with Seneca. According to Thomas Aquinas in his *Summa Theologica*, Gregory of Nyssa argued that anger has a place in the Christian life. Gregory asked rhetorically, "If our anger is quenched, what weapon shall we have against the Adversary?"

I agree with Gregory of Nyssa. I believe it's evident that Seneca's logic is circular. Given Seneca's definition of anger, it's no wonder that he considered it to be useless. In Seneca's opinion, anger is "the most hideous and frenzied of all the emotions . . . the greatest of all ills." He said anger is "temporary madness." Incidentally, the idea of anger as "madness" explains why the English word *mad* is a synonym of *anger.*

Bear in mind, Seneca's view was Stoic, not Christian. Seneca, the Stoic, was born a few years before Jesus. Certain spurious evidence suggests that Seneca corresponded with the apostle Paul. While it's unlikely that he did, it's still conceivable that he did. We know from Luke's account in the book of Acts that Paul spent time with Stoics in Athens (Acts 17:18).

One of the main findings in my doctoral research is that Christian thought has been tainted by the Stoic view of anger. It's a confirmed historical fact that Seneca's three essays *De Ira* (which is Latin for "On Anger") were cut and pasted, so to speak, into Christian textbooks in

Europe for approximately fifteen hundred years. As a result, a long tradition of Stoic teaching took root in Christian thought.

The Stoic influence in the church is still alive today. To give just one example, in the seminary library, I found a 1974 Westminster Press book titled *Overcoming Anger and Frustration*, which offers a disturbing illustration. Author Paul Hauck says that even if you see a person beating a dog, you should not become angry, "because that would be self-righteous." Hauck then adds, "In fact, anger wouldn't arise in the first place if you didn't think you were completely right in your opinion and that the other person was completely wrong." The author echoes Seneca almost verbatim when he says, "All anger is neurotic."

Aristotle

Long before Seneca, there was Aristotle (384 BCE–322 BCE). Aristotle predates Jesus by about three hundred years. Yet Aristotle shaped the thinking of Thomas Aquinas (1225–1274), one of the most prominent Christ followers in church history whose influence to this day is still extraordinary, especially in the Roman Catholic Church.

Aristotle clearly recognized the danger of unreasonable anger, but he also taught that anger is sometimes virtuous. In his *Nicomachean Ethics,* Aristotle said, "Anyone can get angry. But to do this to the right person, to the right extent, at the right time, with the right motive, and in the right way, that is not for everyone, nor is it easy." Aristotle further explained that anger comes in three different measures: an excess amount, a deficit amount, or just the right amount. An excess of anger he called "irascibility"; a deficit amount, "inirascibility"; and just the right amount ("the mean") he called "good temper."

Aristotle discerned that anger is a desire. Gregory of Nyssa, perhaps echoing Aristotle, likewise defined anger as desire. Again according to Thomas Aquinas in his *Summa Theologica*, Gregory said that anger is "the sword-bearer of desire." But Aristotle's definition is more nuanced: "Anger is a desire accompanied by pain for apparent retribution aroused by an apparent slighting against oneself or those connected to oneself, the slighting being undeserved." Put simply, Aristotle viewed anger as a pained response to a perceived injustice that includes a clear wish that the offender will be punished.

Drawing on Aristotle, Thomas Aquinas said something similar: "If one desires the taking of vengeance in any way whatever contrary to the order of reason, for instance, if he desires the punishment of one who has not deserved it, or beyond his deserts, or again contrary to the order prescribed by law, or not for the due end, namely the maintaining of justice and the correction of defaults, then the desire of anger will be sinful, and this is called sinful anger." Evidently, Thomas Aquinas agreed in his *Summa Theologica* that anger is inseparable from desire. Desire has to do with human motives. The "desire of anger," as Thomas put it, should be guided and informed by reason. Thomas believed that reason can harness anger. So you see, Thomas's view is the opposite of Seneca's. Instead of pitting anger against reason, Thomas Aquinas pitted the unreasonableness of sin against reasonable anger.

The Difference between Godly Anger and Sinful Anger

A major theme in Scripture is that God requires God's people to be holy. The principle of holiness applies to everything about us, including our feelings. I believe God wants us to consecrate our feelings and be holy in our emotions as well as our actions.

What is godly anger? In his *Letters to Malcolm*, C. S. Lewis put it this way: "Anger is the fluid that love bleeds when you cut it." Here's my definition: godly anger is the guardian of love. What is the difference between godly and sinful anger? A simple distinction is this: whereas sinful anger opposes love, godly anger opposes love's enemies.

To catalog the differences between sinful and godly anger, I created a Comparative Anger Chart. Can you imagine what might happen if a critical mass of Christians started living out the left side of the chart? I believe the church would be re-salted.

Comparative Anger Chart

Godly Anger	Sinful Anger
Fears the Lord	Fears something other than the Lord
Jealous for the Lord	Jealous out of personal insecurity
Fights the good fight of faith	Fights unfairly for the flesh
Seeks God's interests	Seeks self-interest
Serves God	Serves mammon
Entrusts itself to God	Rails against God
Builds integrity	Compromises integrity
Requires accountability	Evades accountability
Teaches	Taunts
Speaks truth	Speaks lies
Embraces truth	Revolts against truth
Exposes truth	Hides truth
Attempts to heal	Attempts to harm
Stages interventions	Attacks
Inflicts the "faithful wounds" of a friend	Causes damage
Relates authentically	Bluffs
Loves correction	Feels insulted by correction
Appreciates honest feedback	Personalizes critiques
Rebukes	Blames and shames
Disciplines	Punishes

Dignifies	Degrades
Develops people	Exploits people
Protects	Bullies
Listens first	Presumes
Aims to save souls	Aims to save face
Grieves	Sulks in self-pity
Leaves vengeance for the Lord	Takes revenge
Prompted by the Spirit	Quenches the Holy Spirit
Waits on God	Gives up on God
Worships God	Defies God
Loving	Unloving
Truthful	Self-deceived
Sobering	Intoxicating
Zealous	Reckless
Courageous	Feels threatened
Righteous	Self-righteous
Wise	Foolish
Mature	Immature
Proactive	Reactive
Prayerful	Prayerless
Humble	Prideful
Reasonable	Unreasonable
Principled	Unprincipled
Self-sacrificial	Self-indulgent
Short-lived	Harbors bitterness
Corrective and constructive	Condemning and destructive
Hopeful	Cynical
Holy	Unholy
Opposes love's enemies	Opposes love
Guards love	Guards pride

Chapter 3

What Does Jesus' Anger Look Like?

When I began to study Jesus' anger, I was struck by the observation that every time the Bible says Jesus was angry, he's the only one who was. Conversely, every time others were angry, Jesus was not. Only Jesus, for example, railed against the hypocrisy of the Pharisees. Likewise, no one but our Lord was "consumed with zeal" when money changers overtook the temple. It was Jesus, no one else, who generated indignation when his disciples rebuked good parents who brought their children to see the Lord. It was Jesus who rebuked the storm. It was Jesus who reproached his own disciples. Jesus alone groaned when full cities of proud people refused to have faith, even after witnessing his miracles. It was Jesus, no one else, who raged at the tomb of Lazarus. In every situation that drew out Jesus' anger, he alone had the sensibilities to salt the situation with the anger of real love.

"Love your enemies," Jesus said. Thus, he loved them with the love of godly anger.

But Jesus was long-suffering, too. On the night of his arrest, Jesus allowed Roman soldiers to capture him and treat him as a traitor. When rogue authority figures, including the Jewish high priest, pompously framed Jesus as a blasphemer, he stayed silent. Given Jesus' staunch decision to lay down his life for the world, he stayed focused on his mission and let others accuse him falsely of doing the very thing that he was *not* doing, but that they themselves were doing hypocritically. Peter, in stark contrast, apparently became so furious that on the night when the authorities arrested Jesus, Peter lunged to attack them with his sword. Though the Bible only gives hints as to the details of what happened, in my mind it suggests that Peter tried to slay the high priest. Stabbing in the dark, Peter missed the high priest and instead sliced off the ear of the high priest's slave. Jesus, by contrast, stooped down to the ground, picked up the bloody cartilage of the slave's detached ear, and miraculously reattached it and healed him.

"Love your enemies," Jesus said. Thus, he loved them by surprising them with grace.

How often have you and I surprised our enemies with grace? How often have we loved them with godly anger? All of us are guilty of being irascible (too angry) and inirascible (not angry enough). We're angry when we shouldn't be, and not angry when we should be. We're irascible when we hold grudges or lash out at other people, and we're inirascible when we tolerate corruption, especially religious corruption, due to our own selfish lack of zeal.

Jesus was neither irascible nor inirascible. He was neither a Tartar nor a doormat. He was angry and not angry in all the right ways and at all the right times. I marvel at Jesus' anger for a variety of reasons, including the notable fact that no one ever criticized him for it. Isn't that fascinating? Jesus was falsely and unfairly accused of many different things. He was dubbed as a drunkard, a glutton, an insurrectionist, a liar, a bastard, a Sabbath breaker, a criminal, an insubordinate blasphemer, and a demon-possessed member of Beelzebub. But never was he accused of being a hothead.

Godly Anger and Moral Authority

So now, what does that tell us about the nature of godly anger? I believe it says that godly anger is a form of moral authority. Moral authority rests on truth that is transcendent. When anger is infused with moral authority, it displaces selfish pettiness and revenge. Moral anger is deeply principled. Moral anger understands that right and wrong aren't washed away by shades of gray. Moral anger holds high standards and refuses to lower them. It's commanding. It's relentless. It prevails.

Moral anger, as a result, looks like stern leadership. It leads. It does not mislead. Moral anger dares to promote God's standards. Moral anger stands like steel. It isn't tossed by waves of self-preserving doubt or philosophical winds of deception. Moral anger acts out of genuine love for God. Thus, moral anger trumpets one main thing: the unrelenting truth that God is faithful.

This, above all, is what I discovered by examining Jesus' anger: Jesus wants us to rely on God's integrity. Jesus' anger rescues people who struggle to rely on God's total and complete reliability. Jesus' anger tells us that willful unbelief in the honesty of God displeases God. Anytime we sin and refuse to repent, we willfully refuse to trust God. Trusting God is what the Christian life is about. Mind you, we aren't required to trust God blindly or unintelligently or insincerely. But God does require us to have enough trust to submit to divine wisdom and not to human wisdom that is worldly.

Secondly, what I found by observing Jesus' anger is that Jesus was unwilling to compromise his own integrity. Never did he wink at corruption. Never did he falter by joining the ranks of religious leaders who were respectable and impressive, yet faithless and dishonest. Jesus was never dishonest. That is why his faith never failed. I believe Jesus' truthfulness cultivated his faith, and that his faith fueled godly anger, and his anger championed integrity, and his integrity honored truth at every point. See the spiritual principle? The more honest we are ourselves, the more able we will be to trust God. As simple as this may sound, it is revolutionary. If you want to trust God more, then be more truthful. Truthfulness enhances our ability to see that it is *true* that God is utterly reliable.

Thirdly, I noticed that Jesus hated it when God's name was used to hide religious corruption. Let me try to say this yet more plainly. To hide corruption behind God's name is to take God's name in vain. To "play the God card," so to speak, for the purpose of making it seem as though sin is *not* sin is to break the Third Commandment. For example, when religious organizations appeal to religious defenses in order to cover up their abuses, they are blaspheming the holy name of God. To evade accountability in the name of Christianity is anti-Christian. Jesus' anger burned against this type of violation of God's law. He abhorred religious corruption perhaps more strongly than anything else.

Fourthly, to my surprise, I found fifteen different stories in the Gospel accounts that showcase Jesus' anger. These stories are encouraging because they verify the truth that God hates evil more than we do. So often God is scapegoated for allowing sin and evil, but in Jesus' anger we see that God is caring and attentive and just. God knows when you're sinned against, and God hates it. In fact, Jesus died to free you from the forces of all wickedness and evil. He came to rescue you and me from our own waywardness.

Jesus' anger is our medicine. It cures us of our shame. It remedies our wrong thinking by yanking us out of the clutch of mesmerizing lies that skew our thoughts. Jesus' anger is a gift, not a punishment. It's a flash flood warning, so to speak. It's a loving, benevolent warning meant to steer us away from "floods," so we don't drown. Just as floods rain down within seconds, destroying within minutes lovely buildings, fancy cars, and precious human lives, so sin sweeps people away sometimes quickly. Jesus doesn't want you to be swept away by sin. He wants to save you from all sin, including the harsh sins of other people.

I thank Jesus for his anger; it assures us that God's love isn't angerless or toothless or indifferent to the evil that besieges us. "God is a righteous judge, and a God who has indignation every day" (Psalm 7:11). God is angry about the sins that beat you down. God is angry about injustices you've suffered. God's anger is your shield. God's anger is your refuge. God's anger is your pillow to rest upon. I believe God is displeased when any sins at all are committed against you, including when you sin against yourself.

Wouldn't it be terrible if God were lackadaisical about sin? If God yawned when horrors happen? In the sight of horrific sin, God acted in the most dramatic way. God sent his only begotten Son to conquer evil and the sin of evildoers. Then Jesus sent his Spirit to convict the world of sin so that we might turn to God and be transformed.

When we sin, we abase ourselves. Thankfully, Jesus' anger is there to help us slough off abasing things, because you and I are meant to do dignifying things that are glorious. God wants us to judge angels (1 Corinthians 6:3). The plan is for us to co-reign (2 Timothy 2:12; Revelation 22:5). We are meant to become partakers of God's divine nature (2 Peter 1:4). God's redemptive plan is for everyone in Christ to be seated with Christ Jesus on his throne (Revelation 3:21).

Fifteen Stories about Jesus' Anger

I invite you now to join me as I retell stories that feature Jesus' anger during the years of his public ministry. The ordering of the stories is my own. I have numbered them, so you can keep count of them. As I describe them, you will see that I have embellished them with my own imagination. I have thought long and hard about what Jesus' anger felt like to those who were there to feel it and experience it. Plus I know firsthand that there is nothing like Jesus' anger to prompt believers such as me to repent from doubting God.

Story 1: Jesus Confronted the Pharisees

Jesus was angry when he confronted the Pharisees. His anger was sensitive, well reasoned, and pure. Yet it was totally unfiltered by the conventions of restraint that people call "politeness." Jesus was so truthful, so politically incorrect toward the Pharisees that he threw them under the bus, so to speak, by broadcasting their sins in broad daylight. Here's what Jesus said in a public forum:

> The scribes and the Pharisees have seated themselves in the chair of Moses; therefore all that they tell you, do and observe, but do not do according to their deeds; for they say things and do not do them. And they tie up heavy loads, and lay them on people's shoulders; but they themselves are unwilling to move them with so much as a finger. But they do all their deeds to be noticed by people . . . and they love the place of honor. (Matthew 23:2-6, NASB)

Jesus was the ultimate prophet. He did not mince words with platitudinous speech or bureaucratic jargon or vague, misleading statements. Nor did he take pains to prevent himself from being called divisive. Jesus knew he was divisive. He was divisive on purpose. He couldn't have been plainer about that. He told his disciples:

> Do not think that I came to bring peace on the earth; I did not come to bring peace, but a sword. For I came to set a man against his father, and a daughter against her mother, and a daughter-in-law against her mother-in-law, and a man's enemies will be the members of his household. He [or she] who loves his father or mother more than Me is not worthy of Me; and he [or she] who loves son or daughter more than Me is not worthy of Me. And he [or she] who does not take

his cross and follow after Me is not worthy of Me. (Matthew 10:34-38, NASB)

John the Baptist said it, too. When the Pharisees and Sadducees came out to him to be baptized, John the Baptist said to them, "You brood of vipers . . . bring forth fruit in keeping with repentance" (Matthew 3:7-8, NASB). John the Baptist didn't welcome them, even to be baptized, because he knew their hearts were full of treachery. These religious leaders were not interested in God; they were interested in ill-gotten gain. They wanted to be impressive, so they invested in their personas and turned religion into a backroom shady business. John the Baptist saw the truth about who they were. He therefore said to them:

And the axe is already laid to the root of the trees; every tree therefore that does not bear good fruit is cut down and thrown into the fire. As for me, I baptize you with water for repentance, but He who is coming after me is mightier than I, and I am not fit to remove His sandals; He will baptize you with the Holy Spirit and fire, and His winnowing fork is in His hand, and He will thoroughly clear His threshing floor, and He will gather His wheat into the barn, but He will burn up the chaff with unquenchable fire. (Matthew 3:10-12, NASB)

Jesus is going to separate the "chaff" (empty husks) from the "wheat." In other words, Jesus came to expose empty pretenders (chaff). God will not be mocked. It is not OK with God for people to be pretentious and adorn themselves with religion when they operate with deceit and heartlessly wield power over others.

Jesus was disenchanted with the empty-husk religion of the Pharisees of his day. So Jesus called out the problem plainly and simply. How many of us are willing to call out gaping inconsistencies between what is practiced and what is preached in Christian communities?

The Pharisees seemed religious, but they were actually irreligious. They were designated wardens of doctrine unapplied. As if caught up in corporatism, the Pharisees were essentially corporate minded. They rationalized their habit of promoting their own image at the expense of the very mission they espoused. The Pharisees wanted glory, not God. They had big appetites for acclaim, because inwardly they were godless and empty. Their souls were shriveled up. They were withered and parched and dry because they would not receive the love of God.

Their prestige was their religion, and their identity their cash flow. They did not do humble service unto the Lord. Instead, they kept deceiving themselves by patting themselves on the back for being far above the tax gatherers, who exacted money unjustly by demanding higher tax payments than citizens really owed. The Pharisees felt superior because their own systemic way of exploiting naive people was not subject to review by any accountability structure other than themselves and their own cronies. Hypocritically, they sat smugly in their self-justified corruption, which mirrored that of the tax gatherers whom they haughtily despised and denounced.

The Pharisees' problem, at root, was that they wanted to be seated on God's throne—but they didn't want God to seat them. They wanted to seat themselves. And they wanted God even God to bow down to them. How enticing is the trap that the Pharisees fell into! They wanted superiority, not holiness. They wanted religious power rather than the transforming power of love.

In Jesus' righteous anger, he said to the scribes and Pharisees, "Woe to you . . . woe to you . . . woe to you . . . woe to you . . . woe to you . . . woe to you . . . woe to you . . . woe to you!" Eight times in a row in one concise paragraph (Matthew 23:13-32, NASB) he said to them, "Woe to you!" I wonder if Nicodemus, the Pharisee who secretly came to Jesus, was awakened to Jesus' love by hearing these woes. Jesus wouldn't have been so bothered had he not cared about the persons who were Pharisees. Jesus respected them enough to point out the grave distortions in their thinking: "For you tithe mint and dill and cummin, and have neglected the weightier matters of the law—justice and mercy and faith" (Matthew 23:23, NASB).

The Pharisees had lost their sense of proportion. In their passion for the law, they added to the law and then *enshrined* the law such that they became a law unto themselves. The tragedy for the Pharisees was that they believed mistakenly that the law was meant to guide them into an autonomous state of perfection. In other words, the Pharisees wrongly believed that by following certain aspects of the law, such as carefully tithing their spices to exact percentages, they could stand above their need for God's forgiveness. The Pharisees wanted salvation that they could earn themselves. But that is not salvation. Salvation, by definition, is a gift. They didn't want a gift. They wanted glory.

Jesus saw straight through their selfishness. He scathed them for their deceitfulness, saying, "For you are like whitewashed tombs, which on the outside look beautiful, but inside they are full of the bones of the dead and all kinds of filth. So you also on the outside look righteous to others, but inside you are full of hypocrisy and lawlessness" (23:27-28).

Jesus was not dissuaded by how nice these people seemed or how spiritual they appeared. The Pharisees' being well networked and well dressed didn't mean a thing to Jesus. From Jesus' way of relating to the Pharisees of his day, I believe it's evident that God is not impressed by the impressive things of worldly Christianity. In fact, I believe it's evident that worldly Christianity isn't Christianity at all. When I say "worldly," I don't mean earthly. I'm not talking about being earthbound. I'm talking about being fleshly and therefore hostile to God's Spirit (Galatians 5:17). When worldliness creeps into so-called Christian organizations, Christian organizations become less Christian. All professing Christians can degenerate into "Pharisees" when we prioritize appearances at the expense of our own integrity as believers.

To be fair, I need to say that the Pharisees Jesus confronted were only a segment of the sect. Not all Pharisees were imposters in Jesus' day. The problem was not their Pharisaism, but their phoniness. Still today, Christian phonies come in all manner of stripes: some are Christian celebrities who lead empty lives offstage; some are college-level Bible professors who guide impressionable students into doubting God's word even to the point of doubting God; some are priests and missionaries who do unspeakable things to children; some are officers in church denominations who routinely hide misconduct and abuse; some are legalists; some are charismatics doing show business on TV for a lucrative profit; and some are positional leaders in religious institutions who wave a religious flag and hide religious corruption under unchecked religious freedom that disregards religious responsibility.

According to the Scriptures, when people fall into the trap of pharisaical sin, we live by a double standard. We don't practice what we preach. We evade accountability for the purpose of evading authenticity. We aren't honest. We aren't earthy. We refuse to tell the truth about ourselves. Sure, we'll go to John the Baptist to be seen getting baptized, but we will not confess specific sins. The treachery of being a Pharisee in the sense that I mean here is that it causes normal sinners to pretend to have no sins of concrete action. Jesus said to the Pharisees, "You serpents, you brood of vipers, how shall you escape the sentence of hell?" (Matthew 23:33, NASB).

Bear in mind that in Jesus' day, the Pharisees were *not* known as hypocrites. They were credible in the eyes of the unassuming crowd. They looked legitimate with their robes and phylacteries. That is, they seemed like holy people to those who didn't notice that the Pharisees' words were strangely out of line with the Pharisees' actions. From the vantage point of the people who were yearning for the Pharisees' approval, the Pharisees looked just fine.

Jesus wasn't seeking their approval. Jesus was searching hard for their salvation. That's why Jesus said to them in unequivocal terms, "Woe to you, scribes and Pharisees, hypocrites, because you travel around on sea and land to make one proselyte; and when he becomes one, you make him twice as much a son of hell as yourselves" (Matthew 23:15, NASB). What a statement! In saying to them directly, ". . . twice as much a son of hell as yourselves," I believe Jesus gave them the most superlative loving message that he could have conceivably conveyed.

Let's get this straight. Jesus told the Pharisees exactly who they were. He did not falsely accuse them. He announced to them the truth of their identity. In doing this, I believe, Jesus addressed the deepest part of them. He spoke to *them*, not their personas, because personas cannot be saved. Personas are social masks, not human faces. Personas cannot feel, much less repent or receive forgiveness. Thus Jesus cut right through the Pharisees' personas and spoke to them directly as real people. It was a gift for Jesus to talk to them personally, because they (not their personas) were the ones who needed God.

Grief and Past Churchgoers

How many past churchgoers have altogether stopped attending the local church on account of all the "Pharisees" they've encountered in our Christian corporations? Many committed past churchgoers have a long list of legitimate laments. For example, it's not right for kids at church to be mistreated. It's not right for girls to be hit on by their youth pastor. It's not right for teenage boys to be introduced to porn by a church elder. It's not right for men and women to have been suckered into believing that their money was going to poor people when really it was pocketed by someone on church staff.

So many things aren't right. It isn't right for softhearted critics to be punished for contributing sincere, constructive input. It isn't right for eager women to be sidelined when they try to use their gifts. It isn't right for an associate pastor to be fired due to the envy of an insecure senior pastor who is less capable. On and on I could go. Past churchgoers have true stories, and some of their stories are tragic, and all of their honest complaints should be regarded, not disregarded.

The challenge for past churchgoers is to come back and do their part to build integrity. When members just give up on the Christian community, we give in to the status quo. We make things worse. Instead of beefing up the integrity of local churches, we allow them to become yet more anemic. Unintentionally, we deprive the Christian community of integrity that we ourselves could add to it. Instead of strengthening the church with our attendance and zeal, we disconnect. We get fed up. We walk away. Then we ourselves become hypocrites!

Here's what happens: First we feel angry at the "Christians" because the "Christians" aren't acting like Christians; then we ourselves stop acting like Christians because we're mad. So then another set of would-be churchgoers see us outside of church, disconnected and unforgiving, and then they get uninspired at all the private antichurch "Christians" who aren't acting like Christians either. It doesn't take many years before a ton of us evolve into a great big disappointment to each other.

How many Christians or "used-to-be Christians" are so angry that they now feel numb? I believe there are millions. I'm convinced these angry people are very sad. But to whom can they show their sadness when there's no space to grieve? What relational space is there for angry, sad "post-Christians" to weep about the corruption in so-called Christian ministries today? The majority of past churchgoers, at least from what I see, want to kick the church, then leave and not come back. Many want to distance themselves from all things church. Many have lost hope. Many, even pastors, have become cynical.

Jesus wasn't cynical. Yet if anyone ever knew the full reality of the depravity of humanity, it was Jesus. Jesus squarely faced the truth that all of us, each person, from Adam and Eve on down, are afflicted with loveless motives in our hearts. Because Jesus was perfectly honest, he was able to remember that no person in the world is able to be holy without God. Jesus hated corruption more than we do, yet he resisted the temptation to give up on the viability of what can happen when people gather for the purpose of loving God as a group. When people love God truly, everyone gets loved.

I understand the pain of past churchgoers who have been stung by church authorities. I myself have reacted by fretting with sinful anger about the systematic abuses that I know of. Jesus never reacted with sinful anger. He was never disillusioned. Jesus' expectations were totally consistent with reality. Never once was Jesus shocked by the sinfulness and abuse of robed religious clergy or fake religious bigwigs. How did Jesus stay so pure? By entrusting himself to no one else but God (John 2:24). Jesus bore in mind the reality of the condition of every sinner's heart:

There is none righteous, not even one;
　　There is none who understands,
　　　　There is none who seeks for God,
All have turned aside, together they have become useless;
　　There is none who does good,
　　　　There is not even one.
Their throat is an open grave,
　　With their tongues they keep deceiving,
The poison of asps is under their lips;
　　Whose mouth is full of cursing and bitterness;
Their feet are swift to shed blood,
　　Destruction and misery are in their paths,
And the path of peace have they not known.
　　There is no fear of God before their eyes,
　　　　(Romans 3:10-18, NASB)

It's unpleasant to be mindful of the truth of human hearts. But unless you and I are honest about our absolute incompetence to rule our hearts ourselves, we will not be willing to let Jesus rule instead. Every two-year-old in the world wants to rule the world. The pain of pride sets in at an early age. But when we rule our hearts ourselves, we turn into tyrants. It doesn't take long for a self-ruled, fallen human to become a bully. We may bully ourselves either by being way too hard on ourselves or by objectifying other people and forgetting that they share our same humanity. Some people even attempt to bully God.

The point I'm making here is that every self-ruled heart rebels against truth, even when the truth is spoken in love. Jesus was offensive precisely because he spoke the truth in love. Speaking the truth in love is offensive to those who do not love the truth. Love itself is offensive to those who aren't honest enough to accept that love inherently is truthful.

Because Jesus loved the Pharisees, he pointed out the truth of their hypocrisy. That's why he punctuated his indictment of these lawbreakers with loving words of grief: "O Jerusalem, Jerusalem, who kills the prophets and stones those who are sent to her! How often I wanted to gather your children together, the way a hen gathers her brood under her wings, and you were unwilling" (Matthew 23:37, NASB).

Jesus grieved. Unless you and I, too, become willing to grieve, we will not be able to produce the salt of anger that is loving. When my parents divorced, I didn't want to grieve. I didn't want anything sad to be there in existence for me to grieve. I wanted to get rid of that part of reality. I selfishly wanted my parents to hurry up and reconcile, so I wouldn't have to be from a broken family. All that selfishness in my heart produced selfish anger in me.

Some of my anger, however, aligned with God's. For example, I hated divorce with God who hates divorce (Malachi 2:16). I also hated the lies that eroded so much trust in my parents' marriage. Nothing in life consoles me as knowledge of God consoles me—I love it that the

Lord detests lies (Proverbs 12:22). I can't stand it when Christians don't talk or make any concerted effort to work things out in person in open dialogue. Shutting out the truth by shutting out each other is a surefire way to ask for unnecessary defeat.

Why choose defeat when there is hope? All things are possible with God (Mark 10:27). Yes, there is trouble in this world. Jesus plainly said, "In the world, you will have tribulation" (John 16:33, NASB). I didn't want to have tribulation. I did not desire to accept that I couldn't fix things for my family. My parents were the only ones who could possibly build their marriage. I felt helpless. In my raging sense of helplessness, I turned against myself and subconsciously acquired an eating disorder. I rebelled because I didn't like my pain.

Now we're approaching headquarters where sin is manufactured—in people's pain. I learned this the hard way: we have to engage our pain—in humility—or else pain will enlarge our pride and make us perpetrators. Pain latches onto pride and reproduces more pride that is renegade, even violent. From the vantage point of pride, it is painful to be vulnerable, and painful to be honest, and painful to be human, not divine.

Pain and Grief

Just as anger is sinful or godly, so pain is sinful or godly. (Note: I'm not referring to physical pain.) Sinful pain emerges from wounded pride. Godly pain derives from injured love. Jesus' pain was that of injured love. When the Pharisees in Jerusalem rejected him, Jesus engaged his pain in humility. That is, he entered into the humility pain imposes. Pain confronts us with the fact that we are vulnerable, not invincible. Pain forces us either to lie or to tell the truth about who we are.

Unlike Jesus, I pretended *not* to be in pain. I somehow kidded myself into thinking I was fine with my parents' divorce. But I was not. I asked myself unkindly who was I to be in pain when it wasn't even my marriage. I was not the spouse who had been cheated on. My mother was hurt far worse by misconduct that caused their marriage to dissolve. In my misguided assessment, my pain didn't count. So I let my pain take over by taking me to the toilet, where I vomited out my pain in isolation.

It is obvious that I had a big problem, but since I also had real knowledge that God loved me, I found the grace to confess my brokenness. I confessed what was happening in secret; I admitted my selfishness; I came to terms with my phobia of food; I resolved to forgive my parents. I did all of that and more, yet I couldn't find the wisdom to stop censuring my anger. Time and time again, I judged myself relentlessly for being "a fat pig" and for failing to be Sweet Sarah in my heart. In pride, I disapproved of my own anger. So I stayed doubly trapped by two hates: I hated the reality of my parents' divorce, and I hated the reality of my anger.

At that point in my life, I did not know how to give myself permission to express my anger honestly. So I expressed it quite dishonestly by turning it against my own body. My fatness became the culprit, and my skinniness the hero. Ah, my heroic skinniness that people constantly praised. As long as I was skinny, I had guys galore and compliments galore, and both helped to distract me from my anger. I was very disappointed that my parents had split up instead of "fighting the good fight" to stay married. I was also unimpressed by their mutual resignation. I hated their unwillingness to tackle their biggest marriage-busting sins.

My parents had led me to Jesus. They had taught me about God. They had given me a little white Bible as my very first birthday present. They had convinced me of God's love. So how was I to know that my parents were having faith struggles? How was I to guess that my father would one day tell me that he doubts he knew the Lord when I was young? I was way too self-absorbed to consider that my parents couldn't give me what they didn't have themselves.

Little did I know that my anger—which I hated—would later become the lifeline to lead me to the truth. My anger was the most honest thing about me. But since I didn't like it, I sublimated it. I pushed it far down inside my being. I hid it from myself—which was itself a dishonest act. Therefore, hiding it infected me with dishonesty. My dishonesty made me lie about my physical need for food. It made me care about my image way too much. It made me snub my own emotions. It morphed me into my own worst enemy.

It wasn't until I finally faced my anger that I acquired the strength to face the truth. For me, this big transition mostly happened spiritually and internally, but it also took place at a physical level. Physically my face turned from the toilet to the truth. My face faced God's face. That's when I began to be healed. Often when I prayed, I repositioned my physical face. So many times I literally cupped my hand under my own chin and turned my face toward heaven, so as to show my face to God. I still do that. I give my face to God, so God can shine God's love on me directly.

Though I hated my parents' divorce, God used my parents' divorce to deliver me from my own pharisaical bent. All of us are inclined to commit the core sin of the Pharisees whom Jesus railed against. That is, all of us are afflicted with the hell-bent propensity to neglect our human duty to grieve. There is nothing more humbling than grieving. That's why grieving is so difficult. Grieving draws attention to the losses we wish we didn't have. Though everyone I know is skilled at doing self-pity, none of us are competent at being humble grievers.

To grieve in humility means to accept unwanted loss. Grieving is a form of surrender. It's letting go of what is lost. It's saying good-bye to a part of self. It's releasing something utterly without harboring any hidden gripes inside. It's coughing up all feelings of entitlement.

So often, instead of grieving, much less grieving in humility, we refuse to engage the real story of what is. We run to our favorite escapes.

We try to make things better. We deny the painful fact that things aren't better. We conjure up a way to avoid dying to what we lost.

Jesus grieved often. The Bible says he prayed with "loud crying and tears" (Hebrews 5:7, NASB). Because he grieved, he was never pharisaical. Salted are the tears of those who grieve. Grief contains an element of anger. Godly grief contains godly anger. Godly grief protests against unnecessary losses: a child lost in a collision with a drunk driver, a bridge lost to a grenade in a petty political war, an opportunity lost because of the jealous, fragile ego of someone else.

The Pharisees didn't grieve. They weren't honest enough to grieve. Because they snubbed their own pain, they snubbed the truth. People who snub truth become liars. The Pharisees, for instance, lied about themselves by presenting themselves as holier-than-thou. One lie led to another. Next thing you know, the Pharisees lied about Jesus to Pilate and King Herod.

Liars do not know the love of God. That's why Jesus said to the Pharisees, "But I know that you do not have the love of God in yourselves" (John 5:42, NASB). The Pharisees weren't honest enough to trust in God's great love. Foretelling the truthful end of feigned religiosity and unconfessed pained pride, Jesus said to the Pharisees, "Behold, your house is being left to you desolate" (Matthew 23:38, NASB).

Chapter 4

Anger That Justifies Hell

*S*in is a word that most people don't like to hear, but when any of us gets sinned against, we usually want an advocate to know and care and bother to do something about it. Part of the gospel message is that God does do something about it. That is where God's wrath figures in.

In this chapter, I want to focus on the source of God's wrath— which is God's jealousy. This chapter is important because it shows how godly anger is rooted indirectly in God's love.

Many Christians know that 1 Corinthians 13, the Bible's famous love chapter, says nothing about love's anger, much less hell. Instead, it says explicitly that love is "not jealous" (1 Corinthians 13:4, NASB) and love is "not provoked" (13:5, NASB). But now, if God is love and love is not provoked, then how could God ever be angry? And if love is "not jealous," then how can God's wrath possibly be rooted in God's jealousy? And if God is truly all-loving, then why does God allow hell?

Two Kinds of Jealousy

From the start, it needs to be clarified that jealousy (like anger) can be either sinful or godly. Let's look at the major difference between these two jealousies.

Godly jealousy is a component of real love. It's the magnetic part of love that pulls people toward God. In 2 Corinthians 11:2 (NASB), the apostle Paul speaks of the "godly jealousy" he had for the church in Corinth to keep them solely committed to Christ as their "one husband." It makes sense why Paul felt jealous on their behalf—Paul himself had "betrothed" them to Christ as "a pure virgin," but here Paul feared that "as the serpent deceived Eve by his craftiness," so the minds of Christians in Corinth appeared to be "led astray from the simplicity and devotion to Christ" (2 Corinthians 11:2-3).

By contrast, sinful jealousy pushes other people down. The biblical writer James refers to "bitter jealousy" (James 3:14) in the context of describing what is evil. The pattern of bitter jealousy is to attack an innocent person out of sheer hatred. People with bitter jealousy feel victimized by their own internal sense of inferiority, yet notoriously they blame the person whom they admire the very most. Because bitterly jealous people feel dissatisfied with themselves, they try to rise *above* themselves by *lying* about themselves.

Driven by bitter jealousy, King Saul, for example, willfully decided that David was his enemy, not his friend. King Saul's sinful jealousy skewed his judgment to the extent of making him paranoid. Saul was so insecure that his jealousy gave way to hateful attempts of premeditating ways to murder David. Saul lied about David by telling himself that David deserved to be killed. The truth is that David had no intentions whatsoever of usurping King Saul's crown, yet Saul could not believe it. Saul's jealousy made Saul blind to the real truth. Although David was the very best warrior in King Saul's army, Saul regarded David as an enemy of the state. Saul just couldn't believe that a warrior of David's stature could faithfully remain under Saul's leadership. Because Saul didn't trust in God's placement of Saul as king, Saul became a very bad king.

Bitter jealousy had the same big distortion effect on the Pharisees who were envious of Jesus. They were so threatened by Jesus that they delivered him to the Roman government to be executed by way of crucifixion. In truth, Jesus was not the enemy of the Pharisees. Jesus was the *savior* of the Pharisees. But the Pharisees couldn't see that. Their jealousy made it impossible for them to be honest about who Jesus really was. Their jealousy deceived them—just as jealousy always does, since sinful jealousy, by nature, is deceptive. Jealousy in the form of envy is what led to Satan's demise when he fell from heaven.

Satan started out as the glorious archangel, Lucifer. But Lucifer envied God. That is, he envied the *Son* of God. In the deceptiveness of Lucifer's bitter jealousy, he decided it wasn't good enough for him merely to be the highest-ranking angel in all of the heavenly host. Being magnificent and spectacular seemed insulting to the archangel, who could stand for nothing less than to be seated as the very top authority. Lucifer wanted to be God. Lucifer simply couldn't handle the glory of being himself (Isaiah 14:12-15; Ezekiel 28:1-5, 11-19). Because he couldn't stand the truth of who he was, he lied about who he was.

Satan fell from heaven on account of his bitter jealousy of the Son of God. Indeed, hell is the place where everyone is bitterly jealous of Jesus. All who are in hell want themselves, not Jesus Christ, to be Lord of all.

The Jealousy of God

Hell is the place of the most deafening, loud collision in the cosmos. Hell is the place where Satan's *unholy* jealousy collides with God's *holy* jealousy. God's jealousy, of course, is infinitely stronger than Satan's.

Though Satan reigns on earth with bitter jealousy against God, Satan only reigns temporarily (1 John 5:19). In fact, Satan has wrath precisely because he knows that "his time is short" (Revelation 12:12). John Milton had it wrong when his Satan in *Paradise Lost* said it's "better to reign in hell than serve in heaven." Satan doesn't reign in hell (Philippians 2:10-11). Nowhere does the Bible say that Satan reigns in hell.

I have come to realize that *no one* reigns in hell. That's part of what makes hell so hellish. Whereas in heaven each person gets to co-rule with holy God, in hell there is no rule. There's only chaos. Since everyone in hell is unruly, there's no ruler. Hell is leaderless and disorganized. It has no referee.

To reject God as the capital-*R* Referee is to reject the only perfect, righteous judge. Hell is totally hellish because of the rivalry, the envy, the bitter jealousy, the dishonesty of everyone there. Nobody in hell will submit to Jesus. Yet only Jesus can judge righteously. Only Jesus can perfect us.

Unless you and I are perfected, we won't ever be perfect. We certainly are not perfect right now. We need Christ to make us whole. He *will* make us whole if we honestly believe that Jesus is both Savior and Lord. "For God so loved the world that He gave His only begotten Son that whoever believes in Him shall not perish but have everlasting life" (John 3:16, NASB).

It's not mean of God to require us to be perfect. God loves us so much that God the Father gave his only begotten Son to perfect us. God wants to perfect us in Christ so that we will be suitably fit to co-reign with Christ (Colossians 1:8; 2 Peter 1:4). God demands perfection because God cannot settle for anything less than perfection. Yet God is *not* a perfectionist in the human sense of the word. Perfectionists, by definition, are imperfect people imposing standards upon others that they themselves cannot meet. God, by contrast, is perfect. God's perfection thus requires perfection from everyone else in order to maintain God's perfect perfection.

Therefore, God jealously desires the Spirit of Christ in us (James 4:5). God zealously wants the Spirit of *truth* in us. God wants us to be truthful as Christ is. Because of God's integrity, God requires us to be holy as God is (1 Peter 1:16). God's jealousy is for our good. God is *not* jealous in an insecure way. God is jealous in a way that is protective, even marvelous and loving.

Jealousy is basic to God's character. The Lord God's name is "Jealous" (Exodus 34:14). The Lord is also a God of justice, but God's name isn't Justice. Yes, God awards us with justice on account of God's saving grace. Justice was accomplished when Jesus made it just for people to be saved by grace.

Justice is important, and God will not compromise it, but justice can be transcended by God's grace. God's grace covers our sins. It compensates for all our many faults. God's grace is so vast and lavish that it makes up for all the injustices we impose on one another and ourselves.

God's jealousy, however, cannot be transcended. No one can bear to stand before the jealousy of God. "Wrath is fierce, and anger is a flood, but who can stand before jealousy?" is a dramatic rhetorical question asked in Proverbs 27:4 (NASB), and the point of it is to say that jealousy is stronger than anger and wrath. If anger is love's guardian, then jealousy is love's heat. God's love is red-hot heat. It burns with all the passion of the flaming fires of truth that cannot be overcome or extinguished. Thus, in hell the flames of truth remain unquenchable.

The Wrath of God

It occurs to me that God's wrath is often misunderstood because so many people assume that wrath necessarily counters love. The problem, in my opinion, is when God's wrath is misunderstood, God's *love* is misunderstood. Think with me on this. It's true that love is not provoked directly, but jealousy *is* provoked. It is God's jealousy that stirs God's wrath (Deuteronomy 32:16, 21; 1 Corinthians 10:22).

According to King Solomon, the wisest man in all of Old Testament history:

> For love is as strong as death,
>
> . . . .
>
> Its flashes are flashes of fire,
> > the very flame of the Lord.
> Many waters cannot quench love,
> > nor will rivers overflow it . . .
> (Song of Solomon 8:6, NASB)

Love is not what everybody thinks. Love is wild. Love is resilient. Love cannot be forced or restrained. No one can force a person to start loving or stop loving, because love is inherently volitional. Who can tame the power of real love? Love's flashes are the flame of the Lord.

The fiery strength of love lies in the *truthfulness* of the Lord. Love is firmly anchored in truth. For if love were to be dishonest, it would be fake. Who wants fake love? God's love isn't fake. In the words of the apostle Paul, "Let God be found true" (Romans 3:4, NASB), no matter how untrue everyone else may be at times. Part of God's perfection is God's truthfulness. It's the truthfulness of God that necessitates God's wrath.

God's wrath burns against lies. Lies, by definition, are always temporary. They can't last. They won't endure. They have no substance. Lies project claims that don't correspond to reality. Lies are unreality. When unreality is believed, beliefs are unrealistic. It's unrealistic, for instance, to believe God isn't good on account of God's wrath.

Mind you, God is not wrath. Nor are we to be to people of wrath. The apostle Paul says that we were "children of wrath," when we "indulged" in the "desires" of the "body" and "mind" (Ephesians 2:3,

NASB). I repeat: God's wrath is part of God's character, but God is *not* wrath. On the contrary, God is fire, God is light, God is truth, God is love, God is life. See the logical connections? Fire. Light. Truth. Love. Life. Fire is light, and light is truth, and truth founds love, and love feeds life. It is not true, therefore, to say that the more wrath a person has, the more alive that person is. It's true, rather, to say that the more love a person has, the more alive that person is. Because God is love, God is more alive than anyone else.

God is also far more caring than anybody else. God's love is totally caring. It's not indifferent. Indifference couldn't care less. Pure love could not care more. God's wrath, believe it or not, is perfectly caring. Wrath, unlike indifference, throbs with care. Though wrath can be so scary, it's actually not nearly as scary as indifference. The very eeriest criminal is not the wrathful one who commits a crime of passion. The eeriest is the one who cannot feel.

The Injustice of Hell

God is never unfeeling or uncaring. It is caring of God to put a stop to evil. Yes, I know it still seems harsh for God to let human beings enter hell. Hell itself seems evil. But the reason is that we, as fallen people, forget what evil is. Evil is anti-God. It's anti-good. Evil is evil precisely because it steals from what is good. It's parasitic. Subtly evil hides in things like beauty and power and people, and then pretends to be something better than it is. Evil invades the gifts of God while claiming to *be* a gift from God, when in truth it is a destroyer of God's gifts. Evil distorts and devours and devastates. So God is going to destroy all evil in hell.

Yet notoriously people chastise God for allowing hell to exist:

- "The punishment of hell does not fit any crime."
- "Eternal damnation for all unbelievers in world history? No way."

- "Unquenchable torturous fire that torments human beings nonstop forever? That is just too evil to be of God."

In other words, people complain, it seems, because they think hell is supposed to be just. Countless Christians appear to have been taught that it is perfectly fair for God to torture endlessly every person who did not say the sinner's prayer. So many Bible believers honestly seem to think that hideous suffering in hell is a matter of justice.

Scripture, I believe, says something different. Let me try to make this clear: Justice doesn't come in the form of punishment, much less torture. Justice comes in the form of *restoration*. God's justice was administered when God nullified Jesus' death by raising Jesus miraculously from the dead.

Echoing Isaiah, here's how Matthew described it in his Gospel:

Behold, My Servant, whom I have chosen;
    My Beloved in whom My soul is well pleased;
I will put My Spirit upon Him,
    and He shall proclaim justice to the Gentiles.
. . . .
A battered reed He will not break off,
    and a smoldering wick He will not put out,
until He leads justice to victory.
    And in His Name the Gentiles will hope.
(Matthew 12:18, 20-21, NASB)

See what it says? The Bible says that Jesus "shall proclaim justice to the Gentiles . . . until he leads justice to victory." Justice ends in victory, not torture. When Jesus proclaimed justice to the Gentiles, he gave them a gift of hope, not condemnation. The victory of justice is not torture. The justice that Jesus proclaimed was that he would not break off a battered reed or put out a smoldering wick. In other words, the justice Jesus proclaimed was life after death. His justice has to do with salvation. Justice has to do with justification.

The surprise we find in Scripture is that God gives justice to the *elect*. After telling a parable on prayer, Jesus said, "Now shall not God bring about justice for His elect who cry to Him day and night, and will He delay long over them? I tell you that He will bring justice for them speedily" (Luke 18:7-8, NASB). Theologically speaking, there is justice in the blood of Jesus. We know from the book of Leviticus that "life" is "in the blood" (Leviticus 17:11). When Jesus bled for us on the cross, he gave us his life in exchange for our death. The only power in the cosmos that can reverse the power of death is resurrection. Jesus' resurrection produced justice over death, and Jesus' death produced justice over sin.

Justice doesn't come automatically. In this fallen world, what comes to us automatically is *injustice*. All of us are mistreated. God is mindful of how tragic our lives can be. God therefore longs to be gracious to us by granting us his justice in Christ Jesus. Listen to what the prophet Isaiah says:

> Therefore the LORD longs to be gracious to you;
>> and therefore He waits on high to have compassion on you.
> For the LORD is a God of justice;
>> How blessed are all those who long for Him.
> (Isaiah 30:18, NASB)

According to the Most High God, Jesus' singular sacrifice is the only proper sacrifice that can compensate for the sins of any person. What good does it do—in terms of justice—for a sinner to suffer in hell for even five minutes? It does nothing to restore either the person or the people whom that person damaged. Anyone who complains "of hell's punishment being disproportionate" would probably render it "just" for heinous sinners to go to hell for five or ten minutes. But even that is *not* just. It doesn't bring any justice, because raw punishment doesn't pay for any sins. Punishment doesn't bring about restoration.

The reason why hell is everlasting is that residents of hell have no resources for restoring what they owe. They have no power to redeem. They can't undo the damage they have done. They can't right their wrongs. They're justice-less, if you will.

Justice, by definition, pertains to right proportion and restoration. If you break someone's window, justice isn't served if you are punished for breaking that window but the window isn't fixed. For justice to be served, that which is due has to be restored in right proportion to exactly what was lost.

Justice from the Lord is a gift of grace. Apart from the grace of God, justice could never come until the final day of reckoning, because pure justice requires 100 percent restoration of all that has been damaged—which is everything. Sure, justice can be administered on a monetary basis; money lost can be repaid. For example, a $100,000 loss can be fully compensated with $100,000 gain as a matter of justice. But who can restore opportunities that were stolen by someone envious of another? Who can bring out the truth after so many lies have been told and long believed? Who can undo the damage of a broken heart or a raped body or murdered life? Who can provide true justice? Only God.

Justice requires full replacement—an eye for an eye, a tooth for a tooth. Most of the time, replacement is impossible. It takes a creator to bring justice, a creator to replace what can only be replaced by re-creation. Only a creator can replace a real tooth with another real tooth. Only a creator can redeem. Hell prohibits justice because hell rejects redemption outright.

So hell is the place of *injustice*. That's why hell is the place of God's wrath. God's wrath reigns in hell because God is a God of love who hates injustice. All sin causes injustice. It's unjust for any person ever to be sinned against. God has no desire for you to be sinned against. God wants you and me to be restored.

Is hell, then, a place of restoration? No. Hell is where restoration can't happen. Hell is the Great Abyss of total defeat. There is no chance whatsoever for any slight improvement to appear in the opacity of hell. Hell is a place of wrath, and wrath is not restorative. Hell is neither a hospital nor a final therapy session. Nor is hell a recovery program or school to graduate from. Hell is condemnation.

The Longevity of Hell

Why doesn't God get rid of hell altogether? Perhaps someday God will. The Bible implies that hell is a black hole of consumption. It's the place where death itself is put to death. It's where hell itself is consumed. Revelation 20:14 (NASB) explicitly says, "And death and Hades were thrown into the lake of fire."

Could it be that God's anger is "but for a moment," even with regard to hell? God's wrath against Jesus—when Jesus suffered hell—didn't last for any more than three days. Jesus suffered in Gethsemane the night before he died. He suffered yet more in his mock trial. He suffered still more—unfathomably much more—in the process of his crucifixion, especially when he absorbed the wrath of God. Did he suffer still more before he was resurrected?

God alone knows the full extent of Jesus' sufferings, and God alone knows what happened in Jesus' death. For God alone knows what death is; we do not. We don't know what hell is either. Hell is a mystery.

God has revealed that hell is a mystery reflective of other mysteries in God's word. Just as it's a mystery that God at once is three in one, so also it's a mystery that hell at once is three things: a place of endless suffering (Mark 9:48), final death (Matthew 10:28), and ultimate total destruction (2 Thessalonians 1:9). According to the Scriptures, hell is a combination of all three.

God's Vengeance

So then, is God vindictive? To be vindictive means to be selfish rather than just. Here again, I want to be clear: God is a God of vengeance, not vindictiveness. God takes vengeance, not revenge. Remember what Aristotle said (that I mentioned in chapter 2) about vengeance? Aristotle claimed that anger is "the desire to hurt another for the purpose of just vengeance." But Aristotle wasn't talking about God. Nowhere does the Bible say that God has any "desire" to harm people—to torment them—even for the sake of just vengeance.

God's vengeance has to with God vindicating you and me. God's vindication is part of God's goodness. Because God deems it to be totally unacceptable for anyone, ever, in any way at all, to sin against *you*, everyone who has ever harmed you is going to be held accountable. I will say this yet again: God does *not* want you to be sinned against. That's why God is not OK with it when you sin against yourself—or against anyone else. God loves you (and me and everyone) infinitely more than we can imagine.

The highest level, though, of God's vindication is for Jesus Christ, God's Son. Though many misguided critics have falsely accused God of being an abusive father, the truth is that God the Father is by far the most fatherly Father. God the Father vindicated his only begotten Son by raising him from the dead and seating him above all rule and authority and power and by subjecting all things under his feet (Ephesians 1:20-21; 1 Corinthians 15:27-28). In other words, God the Father bestowed the highest possible honor upon his Son.

So you see, God's vindication makes everything right. I believe all of us can tell intuitively that something is terribly wrong, not only in this world, but in us personally, too. To some extent, everybody groans and sighs. We all know that the world would be better if we ourselves were better.

But still, we get hung up on the issue of God's wrath and vindication. In our judgment, it doesn't seem fair for God to punish anybody for eternity in hell. Jesus said that those who enter into hell "will go away into eternal *kolasis*" (Matthew 25:46 NASB). The Greek word *kolasis*, though often translated as "punishment," is better translated, I believe, into the English word *restraint*.

The word *kolasis* is akin to the word *kolos*, which literally means "dock." The verbal form of the word is *kolazo*. The word *kolazo* appears in the book of Acts in the story of Peter and John being detained by the religious leaders for preaching the gospel. In Acts 4:21, the New American Standard Bible (NASB) says, "And when they [the religious leaders] had threatened them further, they let them [Peter and John] go (finding no basis upon which they might punish them) on account of the people, because they were all glorifying God for what had happened." In this passage, the Greek word *kolazo* is translated into the English word *punish*. It makes more sense logically, though, to translate it as "dock" or "restrain," since being restrained contrasts directly with being "let go." See how the passage now reads: "When the religious leaders had threatened Peter and John further, they *let* them *go,* finding no basis upon which they might *restrain* them."

The whole reason the religious leaders threatened Peter and John in the first place is precisely that they wanted the apostles to be restrained. They wanted Peter and John to stop speaking and teaching in Jesus' name. They wanted Peter and John to restrain themselves. But when Peter and John refused to do that, the religious leaders tried to dock them, but the religious leaders couldn't do that successfully on account of public opinion and the fact that they lacked grounds for detaining them.

So is hell the place of punishment, as the NASB translation of the Bible suggests? Or is hell the place of restraint, as the New Testament Greek word *kolazo* in Matthew 25:46 suggests? I believe that hell is the designated place where God restrains demons and unrepentant evildoers. I believe God keeps them at bay. The punishment for people in hell is that they're *docked* there. They're confined. They can't get out.

Hell is a hellhole. Though many people claim that the Christian God is elitist—that God excludes non-Christians in an arbitrary, unfeeling, horrible way, the truth is just the opposite of that. God does not snub people. People snub God. God invites all people indiscriminately on the same terms to enter into joy (Matthew 25:21). God gave his only begotten Son to die "for the whole world" (1 John 2:20).

The person who is snobby is the one who snubs God's gift of God's own self. To reject God is to reject the gifts of God. God has no greater gift to give than the Spirit of Jesus. There's a passage in the New Testament in the book of Hebrews that refers to the payback due to those who insult God's Spirit of grace (Hebrews 10:29, NASB). "How much severer punishment do you think he will deserve who has trampled under foot the Son of God, and has regarded as unclean the blood of the covenant by which he was sanctified, and has insulted the Spirit of grace?"

Here again, the English translation found in the New American Standard Bible points to the concept of punishment. Notice, the Greek word used for "punishment" in this passage is not *kolasis*. The Greek word, rather, is *timorias*, which literally means punishment. Given that this is the only place in the New Testament where the word *timorias* is used, I contend that "the punishment" that God metes out to those who reject God's Spirit of grace is confinement. I believe God confines them away from everything that pertains to grace at all.

To explain what "punishment" the writer of Hebrews is referring to, I first need to make plain something else, as yet unmentioned. Many Christians say they came to faith after hearing about the severity of hell.

Fear of hell, they say, is what converted them into Christianity. In other words, they were so scared of God that they agreed to affirm that "Jesus Christ is Lord." What I aim to point out here is the difference between telling God what you think God wants to hear (even if you don't believe it) and actually loving God.

The foremost commandment in all of Scripture is to "love" God with all your heart, soul, mind, and strength (Matthew 22:37; Deuteronomy 6:5). Logically, we can deduce that since this commandment is the highest commandment, it is the most important commandment to obey. I have wondered if on Judgment Day God will simply separate those who truly love God from those who don't. Loving God is not the same as fearing hell. The act of fearing hell requires no love for God—and no love for anybody else.

So when the writer of Hebrews speaks of "punishment," it occurs to me that the punishment of hell amounts to people being spared of having to love God—or having to love anyone for that matter. If someone utterly refuses to love God—that is, to care to seek God and honor God and enjoy God—then perhaps the most loving thing God can do is isolate that person completely. To be isolated completely from God and God's bountiful grace is to be isolated from every good gift. To me, that isolation sounds like punishment. But to someone who, like Satan, refuses to love God as God is, then hell must essentially be preferable.

How deceived must a person be to prefer hell over heaven? How arrogant must someone be to accuse God or deny God's very existence when the truth is that God's wrath guards God's great love? Godly anger guards God's love. If we don't understand that, we will be insulted by God's love.

The New Testament word that is translated as "insulted" in Hebrews 10:29 is *enubrisas* from the Greek word, *enubrizo*—that is, *en* (a syllable that intensifies the word) and *hubrizo* ("to insult"), from which the English word *hubris* is derived. It's important to point out that *enubrizo* surely does not refer to divine hubris (since there's no such thing). It refers, rather, to human hubris—that is, sheer arrogance. This *enubrizo* belongs to insulters who cast insults at God (just as people at the crucifixion cast vile insults at Jesus).

To insult God's Spirit of grace is to reject the grace of Christ. Saying "no thanks" to Jesus means saying "no thanks" to forgiveness and restoration. It means saying "no, thanks" to life. In effect, it is to lie by saying God's vengeance against evil should not apply to you because you, not Jesus, are the one who is sinless.

So you see, God opposes the proud not because God is prejudiced or arbitrary or unfair. God is none of that. God opposes the proud because the proud refuse to be honest. The proud don't tell the truth about their sins or about God's sinlessness. Defying truth like that in such an outrageous ultimate way makes God's wrath burn.

Is it too much for God to require us to be truthful?

Only a liar would say yes.

Chapter 5

What Caused Jesus to Be Angry?

It isn't said too often, but Jesus did a lot of rebuking. He had a well developed, robust rebuking ministry. To rebuke *(epitimesan) literally means to "beat back." It's a strong word that connotes the idea of anger.* My observation is that Jesus very deliberately reserved his holy rebukes for the sinister and the privileged. He did *not* rebuke social outcasts such as harlots or tax gatherers who knew themselves already to be sinners. Curiously, Jesus instead rebuked demons, religious leaders, and his own disciples.

Story 2: Jesus Rebuked a Demon in the Synagogue

Godly rebukes are acts of love. Demons are not interested in love. Demons cannot see the beauty of real love; they're not honest enough to be capable of that. Demons hate redemption. They don't cheer when a wayward life miraculously turns around. Demons like destruction, not restoration. Their incapacity for goodness makes them too empty to applaud a positive change. That's why Jesus rebuked them. He beat them back. Never did he merely reprove them. To reprove them does no good. To reprove means "to expose." A demon can be exposed yet still hold power. Therefore, demons have to be exorcised or resisted or rebuked. It is futile to offer correction to a demon. Demons are, by nature, irremediable.

The Gospel of Luke includes a story about a man in the synagogue who was possessed by the spirit of an unclean demon. This man cried out with a loud voice, "Ha! What do we have to do with You, Jesus of Nazareth? Have You come to destroy us? I know who You are—the Holy One of God!" (Luke 4:34, NASB).

Luke says Jesus then "rebuked" the demon. Jesus ordered the demon out. He said, "Be quiet, and come out of him" (4:35, NASB). Notice, Jesus said nothing more. He did not take time to teach or explain anything at all to the demon. Nor did Jesus offer the reason of why it was unacceptable for the demon to announce who Jesus was. Rather, with visible authority, Jesus "beat back" the demon's loud question, "Have You come to destroy us?" (4:34, NASB). In other words, Jesus did not get hooked into an unfruitful conversation with this demon. Instead, he powerfully used his anger to exorcise the demon in order to bring healing to a man. The Gospel writer Luke, a medical doctor, was apparently so impressed by Jesus' medical command that he, Luke, carefully pointed out that Jesus healed this man "without doing him any harm" (Luke 4:35, NASB).

The response from other onlookers was pure astonishment. They discussed with one another, "What is this word? For with authority and power he commands the unclean spirits, and they come out" (4:36, NASB). Strikingly, they said nothing about Jesus' anger. The reason for this, in my view, is that his anger was a different kind of anger. His anger was so moral that it looked like moral authority. Anger that holds authority over the demons? Anger that speaks so truthfully that demons can't defy the words said? That's the anger of faith, the anger of love, the anger of hope. That's the kind of anger that heals the world.

Stories 3 and 4: Jesus Rebuked a Fever and Rebuked Demons

As soon as Jesus arose and left the synagogue where he exorcised the demon from the man, he went straightaway to Peter's house, where Peter's mother-in-law was suffering from a high fever. Jesus rebuked that fever (Luke 4:39). As a result, the fever left her. That very day, while the sun was setting, Jesus healed many others as well. As Luke describes it, the demons were coming out and crying out to Jesus, "You are the Son of God!" (Luke 4:41). Jesus then rebuked them, silencing them, because they knew him to be the Christ.

That's three rebukes in a row: He rebuked the demon in the man in the synagogue, the fever in Peter's mother-in-law, and the demons who were rebelling by prematurely revealing who he was. Three rounds of rebuking anger, all of which resulted in correction. The demon-possessed man was delivered from the demon; the mother-in-law with the fever was made well; and the demons who were broadcasting Jesus' unique identity were not allowed to speak anymore.

It's simply not enough to know that Jesus is the Christ. To know he is the Messiah, even to know that he is God, is not the same as being submitted to him in a loving relationship. The demons know that Jesus is God's beloved. They believe that, and they shudder (James 2:19). But they rebel against that truth. They don't want Jesus Christ to be Lord of all. They reject his lordship. But they can't reject it utterly. That's why they are helpless when confronted as Jesus confronted them. Godly anger injects authoritative power into warped situations in which demons have found a cozy place to nest.

Story 5: Jesus Rebuked the Storm

Sometime later, Jesus got into a boat along with his disciples. According to both Mark and Luke, "a fierce gale of wind" arose such that waves of heaving water were breaking over the boat and engulfing them and threatening to drown them (Mark 4:37; Luke 8:23, NASB). Everyone aboard panicked, except Jesus. He was in the stern, asleep on a cushion, until his disciples interrupted to awaken him. They said, "Teacher, do you not care that we are perishing?" (Mark 4:38).

Aroused then from his sleep, he rebuked the wind and said to the sea, "Hush! Be still" (Mark 4:39). And the wind died down, and the sea became peaceful and calm. At the sound of Jesus' rebuke, there came another positive change.

Yet Jesus didn't leave it at that. The more pressing issue, I believe, was not so much the weather as it was the disciples' doubt. So Jesus magnified their doubt in order to help them see the needlessness of their faithlessness. "Why are you so timid?" Jesus said. "How is it that you have no faith?" (Mark 4:40).

Dulled by unbelief, the disciples responded with more fear. In Mark's words, "They became very much afraid" (4:41).

None of them said to Jesus, "You mean, we don't really have to be afraid? You want us to relax? You don't like it that we're timid? Are we frustrating you, dear Lord?" Nobody empathized with Jesus. Not one disciple had the humility to consider how Jesus must've ached when he asked them why they were so timid. No one praised God that Jesus was in the boat them with them. No one thanked Jesus. None of the disciples apologized to Jesus for underestimating him yet again. All were too self-focused. Thus, they distanced themselves from him because he had a power that they didn't understand or have themselves.

"Who then is this, that even the wind and the sea obey him?" (Mark 4:41) they wondered, thinking about power more than truth. When people focus on power rather than truth, inevitably they feel intimidated. Intimidated people tend to do two things: bow down to power (whether that power is legitimate or not) and intimidate other people themselves. Perhaps that explains why Jesus never said, "I am the

Power." He said, "I am the truth" (John 14:6, NASB). Truth sets people free. Truth puts everything into right perspective. Power, by contrast, if overly deferred to, skews people's perspectives. Because power is sheer force, it is something people feel. Power does not require people to think. Whereas truth is unintelligible unless people think, power makes its point without stimulating even a single thought. An electric prodding, for instance, can make the slowest bovine move, whether that bovine is a person or a beast.

Let's think this through together. Anger is a source of power. Psalm 62:11 (NASB) says, "Power belongs to God." No doubt, power is ultimately of God because God is omnipotent. Yet God's power is intertwined with God's truthfulness. God's power is legitimate because it overlaps entirely with truth. Truth is what legitimizes power. Power untied to truth is rogue. Thus, when anger is oriented around power, not truth, anger itself is rogue.

Think about it. The anger of wounded pride is basically the reaction of a bruised ego. Having wounded pride is not a legitimate reason to be angry. Human pride lies. It deceives itself into thinking that I am greater than I am. Pride lies to others as well. So God is opposed to the proud (James 4:6; 1 Peter 5:5). Pride is the root of all sin.

When the disciples reacted to Jesus by being afraid on account of his power, they reacted to his power by becoming intimidated. They became absorbed with selfish fear. That's why they didn't worship him or thank him. That's why their emotions were unloving. Their faithlessness prevented them from trusting God in the storm and from realizing their own power *in* the storm.

That's what happens to us as well. We let pride and faithlessness overrule us. Thus, we lose perspective in the storm. Instead of being like Jesus, who rested in the storm, we panic. Panic-stricken, we then become irrational and accusatory. "Lord," we cry with prideful disapproval, "Do you not care that I'm in pain? Look what you're allowing to happen!"

In other words, we blame. Some of us even blame the living God. We blame anyone but ourselves. In our sin, we refuse to be honest with ourselves about ourselves. Thus, when we are sinning, we forfeit our ability to be truthful about God and truthful about other people as well. We reduce ourselves to beasts. Acting like beasts, we orient ourselves around power, not truth. We follow power, not truth. Consequently, our emotions become sinful.

There is much more I could say, but the bottom-line conclusion is the same in this story as in all the other stories in Scripture: God is faithful. When we know that truth, when we gear our thinking to that truth, we become able to walk by faith in God's unfailing faithfulness. Because of Jesus' perfect faith, he felt the right emotion. He got angry at the storm because the storm spooked his disciples, deceiving them into thinking wrong, demeaning thoughts about God. Faithful Jesus then decided to rebuke the sinister storm that never did scare him one bit.

We can see in Jesus that righteous anger is proactive, not reactive. It is purposeful and God-ward. It is stabilized by its commitment to the truth. It reposes in the truth of God's unchanging character and acts in the fear of the Lord. That's why godly anger is so powerful.

Story 6: Jesus Rebuked James and John

According to Luke's chronology, after Jesus rebuked the storm, there came a day when he resolved to go to Jerusalem:

> And He sent messengers on ahead of Him. And they went and entered a village of the Samaritans to make arrangements for Him. And they did not receive Him because He was journeying with His face toward Jerusalem. And when His disciples James and John saw this, they said, "Lord, do You want us to command fire to come down from heaven and consume

them?" But He turned and rebuked them and said, "You do not know what kind of spirit you are of; for the Son of Man did not come to destroy people's lives, but to save them." And they went on to another village. (Luke 9:52-56, NASB)

What stands out most to me in this narrative is the very striking difference between Jesus and his disciples, James and John. Whereas Jesus made no hint of feeling any type of misgivings toward the people who refused to receive him, James and John felt so insulted that they plotted to annihilate a whole village. James and John had wounded pride. In their pride, their hearts caught flame with sinful anger.

Bear in mind that James and John were both enrolled in Jesus' "school," if I can call it that for the sake of making a point. They were his students. They were there in the boat when Jesus rebuked the storm. They were also present on a totally different occasion when Jesus explained the power of mustard-seed-sized faith. Jesus said that faith can move a mountain. Thus, James and John took it seriously when Jesus said that "nothing will be impossible for you" (Matthew 17:20).

So now, on the one hand, it's amazing that James and John believed that they themselves could call down fire from heaven. That's the evidence, in my view, that they had actually been paying attention to their teacher. But on the other hand, they seriously missed the point. Jesus' point was not to issue them a license for moving mountains, so they could crush whole villages of people. His point was to inform them of the power of their faith if they put their faith in God and God's agenda.

Godly anger lobbies for God's agenda. Sinful anger, by contrast, vies for human agendas that may seem justified but are not. When James and John decided they wanted to do away with the Samaritans who refused to welcome Jesus, they weren't thinking about the Samaritans as human beings, as beating hearts. As I imagine it, they were thinking about "those punks;" so James and John dehumanized "those punks" and turned them into "no one" ideologically. That's the operative nature of sinful anger. Cruelly, it dehumanizes people—not only the victims, but the perpetrators. Ironically, in their anger, James and John dehumanized themselves. That's why Jesus rebuked them—to save them from themselves. In one fell swoop, he saved the Samaritans and also two disciples.

Herein lies the genius of Jesus' godly anger: it corrected sinful anger. Whereas James and John were probably thinking, "How dare those Samaritans!" Jesus was probably thinking, "How dare James and John!" So he rebuked them. He beat back their rebellion. Yet he did so with great patience and instruction (2 Timothy 4:2). Rabbi Jesus let them know that they actually *didn't know* what kind of spirit they had given themselves over to.

These two disciples were harboring murderous anger; they were murdering Samaritans in their hearts. They had the vilifying anger that Jesus warned against in Matthew 5:22 in his Sermon on the Mount. Vilifying anger seeks vengeance. God says, "Vengeance is Mine" (Romans 12:19, NASB).

Story 7: Jesus Zealously Cleansed the Temple

This next story is not a story of God's vengeance; it's a story of God's grace. It's by far the most famous story of Jesus' anger. This narrative is recorded in all four Gospels, yet none of the gospel writers mention the word *anger* in it. Scholars therefore debate whether Jesus was angry or not. I, for one, believe that he certainly was. According to the wording in Scripture, when Jesus cleared the temple, he was "consumed with zeal" for his Father's house (John 2:17, NASB). From the apostle John's description, it appears that Jesus' zeal was demonstrably demanding— unyielding and resolute.

The temple was a sacred space for prayer. But the buyers, sellers, and moneychangers converted God's house of prayer into a house of merchandise that operated for the sake of ill-gotten gain. Jesus wasn't merely half-attentive to the irreverence he discovered in God's house. Jesus was "consumed" with zeal. His jealousy for God—that is, his zealousness for God—moved him to take action against all the religious imposters in the room.

According to the Gospel of John, Jesus "made a scourge of cords and drove them all out of the temple, with the sheep and the oxen, and poured out the coins of the moneychangers and overturned their tables" (John 2:15, NASB).

Jesus drove them out all by himself.

I wonder if there were bouncers in the temple. I would think, with all that money right there in the room, that someone would be stationed to guard the place. Yet no one tackled Jesus or ganged up on him to kick him off the property. Instead, Jesus ousted them. Jesus boldly dumped their coins onto the floor and then sent the sellers out without their money. Can you imagine greedy sellers, dressed in respectable garb, physically running out of the temple with their robes disheveled? On account of Jesus' anger, the merchandisers fled.

With no sword, no gun, no military tank, no sidekicks on his team, no help from fiery angels, no nothing but a homespun whip, Jesus cleared the temple singlehandedly. As I see it, Jesus must have been like a she-bear that scares everyone but her cubs. Almost instantly, it seems, Jesus got the wrong people out of the temple and the right people in.

As unrepentant sinners were spilling out of the room, the blind and lame poured in. Children poured in, too. What a marvel! Hardened hearts were repelled, and soft hearts were attracted—all in the same scenario. Matthew puts it this way:

And Jesus entered the temple and cast out all those who were buying and selling in the temple, and overturned the tables of the moneychangers and the seats of those who were selling the doves. And He said to them, "It is written, 'My house shall be called a house of prayer'; but you are making it a robbers' den." And the blind and the lame came to Him in the temple, and He healed them. But when the chief priests and the scribes saw the wonderful things that He had done, and the children who were crying out in the temple and saying, "Hosanna to the Son of David," they became indignant. (Matthew 21:12-15, NASB)

Clearing out the temple mattered to Jesus. Jesus said, "Take these things out of here! Stop making My Father's house a marketplace" (John 2:16, NASB). Here Jesus was alluding to Jeremiah 7:11, which is connected to all the preceding verses in Jeremiah 1–6. The prophecies of Jeremiah were given to "faithless Israel" and "false Judah" (Jeremiah 3:11, NASB). God lovingly called out to them, "Return, O faithless children; I will heal your faithlessness" (3:22). God's caring anger burned against Jerusalem, because in it people said, "As the Lord lives," yet they swore falsely in God's name (5:2). They stubbornly refused to repent (5:3). They were "well-fed lusty stallions" (5:8). "They acted shamefully; they committed abomination; yet they were not ashamed; they did not know how to blush" (6:15). For Jesus, it was intolerable to see such "well-fed lusty stallions," such hard-hearted religious leaders serving mammon in the house of God. Prior to his clearing the temple, Jesus told his disciples, "No one can serve two masters. . . . You cannot serve God and mammon" (Matthew 6:24, NASB).

By clearing out the buyers and sellers and moneychangers, Jesus made it clear that serving mammon is unacceptable, especially in God's house. No church, no Christian ministry, no religious organization should ever prioritize money above God. That kind of prioritization is idolatrous, even apostate. It therefore kindles Jesus' anger and jealous love.

Story 8: Jesus Became Indignant at His Disciples

Scripture does not tell us whether Jesus' twelve apostles or any of his other followers had managed to keep up with him in order to watch him enter and clear the temple. But still, it is safe to say that all of Jesus' disciples were tacitly taking anger lessons specially from him. None of Jesus' students, however, were quick to comprehend the spirituality of his unpredictable anger. After all, nothing that made them angry angered Jesus. Whereas the disciples saw themselves doing a favor for Jesus, for instance, when they shielded him from swarms of babies and children, Jesus took offense at their intervention. Mark's Gospel offers this concise report:

> And they were bringing children to Him so that He might touch them; and the disciples rebuked them. But when Jesus saw this, He was indignant and said to them, "Permit the children to come to Me; do not hinder them; for the kingdom of God belongs to such as these. Truly I say to you, whoever does not receive the kingdom of God like a child shall not enter it at all." And He took them in His arms and began blessing them, laying His hands on them. (Mark 10:13-16, NASB)

Jesus was delighted to be bombarded by little kids. All the laughing, clapping, dancing, talking, cheering boys and girls enlivened him with indescribable joy. Jesus was beside himself, so thrilled by the children's willingness to believe. Faith comes easily to children. They're open to the realm of the supernatural. In fact, it's sensible to them to think a supernatural God would do supernatural things. What else would a real

God do? Kids aren't loaded down with all the weighty rationalizations that are used by boastful people to discredit and explain away God. It's no problem to little kids for God to be invisible. To them, the idea of God makes perfect sense. Jesus understood that. He celebrated that. He recognized that preschoolers don't make good atheists. They're just too honest. So when yet another parent released another set of kids to tackle Jesus with another set of bear hugs, he outstretched his arms to embrace them.

From the point of view of the disciples' incompetent management theory, Jesus was getting a bit too carried away. He had that tendency, you know. He wasn't always strategic as they saw it. Why was Jesus having so much fun? Given the urgency of his ministry, how could he accept another drippy, wet-mouthed baby? How could he make more space to cuddle a toddler or an infant when all these chirping, birdlike children were landing and alighting on his lap? How was anything important ever going to get done with all this chattering and hovering and fluttering?

Perhaps emboldened by their adult sense of importance, being that they had disciple status, the disciples muscled up and rebuked the imposing parents, policing them to move back and get their kids out of the way. But surprise! Jesus didn't like that idea. He became indignant with them.

The Greek word for "indignant" is *aganaktasen* (from the root *aganakteo*), which literally means "to have much grief." Here's the breakdown of the syllables: *agan* (meaning "much") and *achthos* (meaning "grief"). I believe Jesus felt grieved by his disciples' disregard for little ones.

Angry Jesus, though, did not gripe at his disciples. Rather, he mentored his disciples. He corrected them, even in the presence of the babes, kids, and parents. He explained to them that children are actually good exemplars for adults. That is one of the ironies of God's kingdom and of this story. The very children whom the disciples had intended to dismiss were the people whom Jesus pointed to as role models.

Story 9: Jesus Rebuked Peter

Jesus' love was truthful, not polite. To be polite is to be polite-ical. Political. Jesus didn't relate to other people in a political kind of way. Why should he? He wasn't scared. He didn't feel guilty. He wasn't selfishly ambitious. His continual ambition was to please God.

Because he wasn't trying to win the shallow favor of shallow people, Jesus was free to love them instead. He regarded people's souls. He was interested in their destiny. He cared about the condition of their hearts. Jesus wanted people to have abundant life, and since that can only happen when people trust the Lord, Jesus coached his disciples and the Pharisees alike to stop committing the sin of doubting God.

When Jesus began to show his disciples that he must go to Jerusalem, and suffer many things from the elders and chief priests and scribes, and be killed, and be raised up on the third day, Peter fell into a trap. Without realizing he was sinning, Peter "took him aside and began to rebuke him" (Matthew 16:22, NASB). With the same good intentions that pave the road to hell, Peter said to Jesus, "God forbid it, Lord! This shall never happen to You!" In other words, Peter's pride made him presumptuous and caused him to react to the sovereign plan of God by beating back Jesus' willingness to fulfill it.

In response to him, Jesus physically turned around. Matthew says he "turned" (16:23). Jesus turned his body directly toward Peter's. Imagine the contrast. Whereas Peter took Jesus aside and presumably stood next to him shoulder to shoulder, Jesus positioned himself toward Peter face-to-face.

Then Jesus rebuked him, saying, "Get behind Me, Satan! You are a stumbling block to Me; for you are not setting your mind on God's interests, but man's" (Mark 8:33, NASB).

I get a pit in my stomach thinking about this scene. When Peter rebuked Jesus, Jesus rebuked him back. How silencing was *that*?

If you think about it, saying "no" and "Lord" to Jesus, all in one breath, does not make logical sense. Yet I empathize with Peter, even though I realize Peter was sinning. How gut-wrenching would it be to watch Jesus, of all people, be mistreated?

"God forbid God's plan!" is what Peter said, in effect. His words were so emotional they were irrational.

That's what sinful anger does to people. As the Stoic philosopher Seneca said, it seizes them with "temporary madness." Sinful anger is senseless. It makes us stubbornly say no to things we should say yes to. It says "No!" to submitting to God. It says "No!" to sovereign things that stab our egos. It says "No!" before it even knows what it rejects. Sinful anger simply doesn't listen. It's presumptuous. Filled with hubris. Willfully deaf.

Godly anger, by contrast, has good hearing. It is teachable. It is open to hearing more truth. Unlike sinful anger, which acts arbitrarily, godly anger operates with purpose. It is mindful. It's productive. It bears fruit. Godly anger stages interventions. Most addicts don't feel loved when surrounded by family and friends who are spotlighting their addiction, pointing out their destructiveness, and asking them to enter into rehab. But that's because those addicts are still drunk. They're too buzzed and intoxicated to be grateful. Godly anger, regardless, isn't sidetracked. It overlooks ingratitude and sets its face like flint toward restoration.

When Jesus rebuked Peter, he didn't rebuke him in private. He staged an on-site public intervention. Instead of saving Peter's face, Jesus rebuked him face-to-face. I believe Jesus did this because that is what it means to stage an intervention—to intervene "onstage" so that Peter and everyone else there could learn in that same moment what Jesus was about to teach Peter. After saying to him, "Get behind Me, Satan!," Jesus said, "You are a stumbling block to Me; for you are not setting your mind on God's interests, but man's" (Matthew 16:23, NASB).

Peter's problem is emblematic of our problem. We all have trouble listening well to Jesus. We all have selective hearing. We all tend to jump to premature conclusions, especially when we feel threatened personally. Peter wasn't listening fully to Jesus. Once he heard the words "suffer" and "be killed," he kicked into high-gear revolt. Peter didn't have the patience to hang with Jesus long enough to listen to the rest of what he said: "And after three days, rise again" (Mark 8:31, NASB).

Peter missed the high point. He missed what put the rest into perspective. How many times have you and I missed the high point? How often have we reacted before hearing someone out and checking to make sure we really heard them? How often have we replaced the truth of actual facts with the distortions of our own personal insecurities? How often are disputes based on silly misunderstandings? How often is due process not afforded? How many countless people are seriously damaged on account of weak positional leaders who impose their own agendas instead of taking to heart the interests of God?

Peter's heart was wrong. His heart was almost right, but it was wrong. The torturous thought of Jesus being killed by bullying bureaucrats sent Peter through the roof. He couldn't stand it. Because his heart was set on himself, on his own agenda for Jesus, Peter recklessly rebuked the Lord of Lords. In his emotional impetuosity, Peter failed to listen because he failed to be respectful enough to listen. That's the nature of sinful anger—it's disrespectful.

Peter's rebuke of Jesus amounted to a selfish reaction. By contrast, Jesus' rebuke of Peter amounted to a protective proclamation. Jesus' action was not a reaction. He was not one-upping Peter. He was forwarding the interests of God.

Godly anger champions the values and interests of God. It thus upholds core values such as righteousness and love. As the guardian of love, godly anger is protective, even of the *suffering* of love.

So Jesus summoned the multitude along with his disciples. Physically turning back toward them after having his round with Peter, he taught everyone what it means to let go of selfish interests and champion the interests of God: "If any want to become my followers, let them deny themselves and take up their cross, and follow me. For those who want to save their life will lose it; and those who lose their life for my sake will find it. For what will it profit them if they gain the whole world, but forfeit their life? Or what will they give in return for their life?" (Matthew 16:24-26).

But that is not all he said. In addition, he assured them—he assured Peter—that justice was imminent and that God is interested in justice and right rewards: "For the Son of Man is going to come in the glory of His Father with His angels; and will then recompense every person according to his or her deeds. Truly I say to you, there are some of those who are standing here who shall not taste death until they see the Son of Man coming in His kingdom" (16:27-28).

In stark contrast to Peter, who felt threatened by God's interests, Jesus took security in them. Jesus was convinced, even while hanging on a cross, that God's interests are benevolent. Jesus understood that everything works out best when God's interests are promoted, not blocked. Though Jesus had to die, he still trusted God the Father, because he fully believed that God is greater than death. Unless we follow Jesus— walking behind him, not ahead of him—we will not have eyes to see his faithfulness.

Chapter 6

Why Did
Jesus Rage?

U ntil I did my research, I had no idea that Jesus raged. I knew that he had wept. That's the shortest verse in the Bible: "Jesus wept" (John 11:35, NASB). But it stunned me to discover that what happened when Lazarus died is that Jesus raged, then he wept, and then he raged again.

Story 10: Jesus Raged at the Tomb of Lazarus

According to the Scriptures, here's how the story began:

> Now a certain man was sick, Lazarus of Bethany, the village of Mary and her sister Martha. Now it was the Mary who anointed the Lord with ointment, and wiped His feet with her hair, whose brother Lazarus was sick. The sisters therefore sent to Him, saying, "Lord, behold, he whom you love is sick." But when Jesus heard it, He said, "This sickness is not unto death, but for the glory of God, that the Son of God may be glorified by it." Now Jesus loved Martha, and her sister, and Lazarus.

When therefore He heard that he was sick, He stayed then two days longer in the place where He was. (John 11:1-6, NASB)

Imagine the situation: a crisis. Lazarus was dying. Yet Jesus, of all people, refused to visit him. That did not make sense to Lazarus's sisters, Mary and Martha. Jesus, who had a miraculous healing ministry and went around healing thousands, chose not to heal his friend. Mary and Martha were beside themselves. Their brother, their lifetime companion, just couldn't hold on any longer. In a matter of seconds, he was with them and then gone—no more breathing, no more blinking, no more squeezing his sisters' hands. Lazarus had drifted far away. He was sleeping as he had never slept before. The sisters could hardly bear to look at their lifeless sibling. And what made it even more awful was that Jesus could have stopped it, but Jesus hadn't heeded their urgent message.

Had Lazarus been old and decrepit, his death might have been easier to accept. At least then there would have been no one to blame. But Lazarus's death was premature. He was young. He had been sick, and his body provided physical symptoms of warning that made it evident in advance that Lazarus was in danger and needed medical help immediately. In a word, it was obvious to Martha and Mary that Lazarus's death had been *avoidable.*

Why didn't Jesus hurry to come save him? When the centurion's servant was dying, Jesus healed him right away (Matthew 8:13). But when Jesus received the message about his friend Lazarus, he delayed. From Mary and Martha's perspective, Jesus tarried too long. He waited two full days even before setting out to come see them. The gospel account further says this:

Then after this, He said to the disciples, "Let us go to Judea again." The disciples said to Him, "Rabbi, the Jews were just now seeking to stone You, and are You going there again?" . . . And after that He said, "Our friend Lazarus has fallen asleep, but I go, that I may awaken him out of sleep." The disciples therefore said to Him, "Lord, if he has fallen asleep, he will recover." Now Jesus had spoken of his death, but they thought that He was speaking of literal sleep. Then Jesus therefore said to them plainly, "Lazarus is dead, and I am glad for your sakes that I was not there, so that you may believe; but let us go to him." Thomas therefore, who is called Didymus, said to his fellow disciples, "Let us also go, that we may die with Him." (John 11:7-16, NASB)

From the disciples' perspective, it was definitely best for Jesus *not* to go to Bethany. The disciples were relieved that he at first chose not to travel. Journeying through Judea (where the village of Bethany was) sounded suicidal to them. So it was unnerving from their perspective, when merely two days later Jesus suddenly announced, "Let's go to Judea." What were they to do? After all, reasoning with Jesus wasn't easy. Jesus never seemed to catch on to the practical rhythm of the here and now. He always seemed to march to the beat—or maybe the offbeat—of an entirely different drum. In this case, for instance, the disciples were thinking in practical terms of keeping Jesus alive, whereas Jesus was thinking in arrhythmic terms of visiting someone dead.

"So that you may believe." That's what Jesus said. But all the disciples heard was "Let's go to him. Let's go to Judea." In other words, they just heard the crazy beat that Jesus kept marching to.

Missing Jesus' message, Thomas said vaingloriously, "Let us also go, that we may die with him!" This very statement, Thomas's rallying cry, as bold as it may seem, actually exposed his unbelief. The story line is subtle, but it vividly reveals that Thomas was more convinced of the power of the Jews than he was of the power of Jesus. Thomas was more certain that the Jews could kill Jesus than that Jesus could raise Lazarus from the dead.

No one in this story trusted Jesus.

How peculiar that, on the one hand, the disciples took Jesus' figurative language literally by assuming that Lazarus was literally asleep. Yet on the other hand, they took his literal words figuratively by assuming that his prior comment, "This sickness is not unto death," couldn't have meant what it sounded like it meant—that Lazarus's sickness wasn't going to end in physical death.

Consider another segment of the story:

> So when Jesus came, He found that he [Lazarus] had already been in the tomb four days. Now Bethany was near Jerusalem, about two miles off; and many of the Jews had come to Martha and Mary, to console them concerning their brother. Martha, therefore, when she heard that Jesus was coming, went to meet Him; but Mary still sat in the house. Martha therefore, said to Jesus, "Lord, if You had been here, my brother would not have died. Even now I know that whatever You ask of God, God will give You." Jesus said to her, "Your brother shall rise again." Martha said to Him, "I know that he will rise again in the resurrection on the last day." Jesus said to her, "I am the Resurrection and the Life; he who believes in Me shall live even if he dies. . . . Do you believe this?" She said to Him, "Yes, Lord, I have believed that You are the Christ, the Son of God, even He Who comes into the world." And when she had said this, she went away, and called Mary her sister, saying secretly, "The Teacher is here, and is calling for you." And when she heard it, she arose quickly and was coming to Him. Now Jesus had not yet come into the village, but was still in the place where Martha met Him. The Jews then who were with her in the house and consoling her, when they saw that Mary rose up quickly and went out, followed her, supposing that she was going to the tomb to weep there. Therefore, when Mary came where Jesus was, she saw Him, and fell at His feet, saying to Him, "Lord, if You had been here, my brother would not have died." (John 11:17-32, NASB)

The Bible doesn't say if Jesus' initial reply, "This sickness is not unto death," was relayed back to Mary and Martha. I'm convinced, however, that it was. The message must have found its way back to the sisters, along with further word later that Jesus was coming to Bethany, because Martha went out to meet him well before he arrived at her home.

On any other day, Martha probably would have greeted Jesus warmly. But on this day, she did not. Instead of welcoming him with gratitude or relief for his safe arrival, she greeted him with a soulful confrontation, "Lord, if you had been here, my brother would not have died." What she said to him in effect was "Jesus, you're too late." When Mary went out to greet him, she said to him the very same thing, "Lord, if You had been here, my brother would not have died."

Notice what the sisters did *not* say. They did not say, "Lord, if you had been here, Lazarus, whom *you* love, would not have died." Nor did either of them say, "Lord, if you had been here, *our* brother would not have died." Instead, each sister said "my": "Lord, if You had been here, *my* brother would not have died." Martha and Mary alike were caught up in the pain of personal loss.

When Jesus saw Mary and the Jews who came with her weeping, a wave of deep emotion flooded through him. The New American Standard Bible (which is the English translation of the Bible that I used in my research) says that Jesus was "deeply moved in spirit" (John 11:33). The original Greek, however, says that Jesus "raged." The Greek word is *enebrimesato* (from *embrimaomai*), which literally means "to snort with anger like a horse, or to rage."

Why don't our English Bibles reflect the Greek? I believe that is due to the long-term Stoic bias in church history. As I explained in chapter 2, Seneca's non-Christian Stoic teachings were cut and pasted into Christian textbooks for fifteen hundred years—maybe more.

Bearing that in mind, it's important to point out that in Mark 14:5, a form of the same Greek word *embrimaomai* occurs—not with reference to Jesus, but rather to the people who were upset that a woman had "wasted" costly perfume by pouring it lavishly over Jesus' head in preparation for his imminent burial. In that instance, the New American Standard Bible says they were "scolding" (*enebrimonto*) her.

See what I'm saying? When the word *embrimaomai* is used of people scorning a woman for worshipping God, the translators make it plain that *embrimaomai* has to do with anger. But when the very same word is used of Jesus, that Stoic influence says that Jesus, sinless Jesus, could not possibly have raged at Lazarus's tomb. After all, Stoicism teaches that anger is always bad. So from the vantage point of Stoicism, how much worse is rage?

When I first observed this omission—this failure to tell English readers about Jesus' rage—I raced into the commentaries to see if any other scholars had ever noticed this. They had noticed it. Luminaries such as Rudolf Bultmann, Raymond Brown, D. A. Carson, and A. T. Robertson all talk about it in their commentaries on the Gospel of John. All of them acknowledge that the apostle John says twice that Jesus snorted like a horse with anger. Here are the two texts from John 11 (NASB):

He was deeply moved [*enebrimesato*] in spirit. (v. 33)

Jesus, therefore again, being deeply moved [*embrimomenos*] within . . . (v. 38)

Take note, Jesus did not do this outwardly. He did it inwardly. He raged inwardly "in spirit" (*toi pneumati*) in verse 33, and raged inwardly "in himself" (*en heautoi*) in verse 38.

Consider the contrast. He expressed zeal in an *outward* way when he cleared the temple and raged in an *inward* way at the tomb of Lazarus. There, on-site with Mary and Martha, Jesus expressed his anger along with tears. He didn't knock anything down or drive anybody away as he did when he cleansed the temple. But he did do something dramatic. Inside he was exploding with rage.

The question, of course, is this: What was Jesus angry about? Why would the sight of bereaved men and women weeping at the loss of their friend send Jesus into a rage? Who was he angry at? Mary and Martha? Mary and Martha's friends? His own disciples? Was he angry at God the Father for not directing him to visit Lazarus sooner?

I believe Jesus was profoundly enraged at the two primary things that deceptively turn people away from God: death and unbelief. How many people scorn God after death devours somebody they love?

- "God let my baby die!"
- "God could have saved my father, but he died anyway."
- "God took my friend away!"

How many turn against God, blaming God, when the problem is their own unbelief?

- "If God truly loved me, God never would have let this happen!"
- "There can't be a God, because there is too much evil in the world."
- "If there really is a God, God certainly isn't trustworthy."

I am thoroughly convinced that Jesus raged at the tomb of Lazarus because no one, not one person, including Mary or Martha or his disciples, gave Jesus or his Father the benefit of the doubt in the face of Lazarus's death. Death distracted them. It contaminated them. It infected them pandemically with the serious disease that I call "rocks-in-the-heart unbelief."

Death is the "last enemy" because nothing in the world produces unbelief and reproduces faithlessness like death does. As the apostle Paul explains it, "The sting of death is sin" (1 Corinthians 15:56, NASB). To me, Paul's phrase seems backward. It seems like Paul would say, "The sting of sin is death," meaning that sin leads to death, since "the wages of sin is death" (Romans 6:23). But Paul says that death has a stinger—sin.

At the tomb of Lazarus, everyone was stung with selfish dissatisfaction in the God who had let Lazarus die. Nobody believed what Jesus had said to them plainly. All of them complained. All of them lost hope. All of them resigned themselves to defeat.

"Lord, if You had been here, my brother would not have died," said each of Lazarus's sisters. "Could not this man . . . have kept [Lazarus] from dying?" said others who doubted Jesus' goodness and trustworthiness. The death of Lazarus made mourners faithless, and their faithlessness made them blind.

No one had eyes to see what Jesus was doing because no one had ears to hear what he had said. In plain, straightforward language, Jesus had preannounced, "This sickness is not unto death."

Not unto death.

Not.

He had used the word *not*, but nobody had heard him. Death and unbelief had stolen at least two of their five senses. I believe Jesus hated that. To be clear, the problem wasn't their weeping. Jesus wept, too, but apparently not when the others did. A close look at the Bible shows that when Jesus saw Mary weeping and the Jews who came with her also weeping, that's when Jesus raged: "When Jesus therefore saw her [Mary] weeping, and the Jews who came with her also weeping, He raged [*enebrimesato*] in spirit, and was troubled, and said, 'Where have you laid him?' They said to Him, 'Lord, come and see.' Jesus wept. And so the Jews were saying, 'Behold, how He loved him!' But some of them said, 'Could not this man, who opened the eyes of him who was blind, have kept this man also from dying?' Jesus therefore again, raged [*ebrimomeno*] within, [and] came to the tomb" (John 11:33-38, NASB).

As the narrative is described, Jesus didn't weep until after he was led to the tomb. What stands out to me in this story is that when Jesus started weeping, the others *stopped* weeping. Apparently everyone was struck by the way that Jesus cried. "Behold, how He loved him!" they said.

My theological sense is that Jesus' crying was different because Jesus cried for Lazarus, not himself. In his compassionate wisdom, Jesus understood that Lazarus was about to be summoned to depart from the presence of the One to whom Jesus prayed. Only Jesus knew the pain of leaving heaven (John 1:1, 14). Only Jesus knew the experience of saying good-bye to God the Father when he, God the Son, became flesh (John 1:14, 18). Moreover, Jesus uniquely had the foresight to be sad, knowing that after Lazarus was raised from the dead, Lazarus would have to die again.

The actual act of dying is unlovely. Dying is a departure from this present life. Dying is a passing that, on the one hand, is a relief but, on the other hand, is a consequence of sin. I believe that Jesus raged against that consequence—because death is a thief that not only steals life, but also tends to rob people of faith.

The tomb was a cave, a burial cave, sealed with a burial stone. As I envision it, all anyone could see at the mouth of the cave was a cold, impersonal rock that imposed a final barrier between the people and their friend Lazarus. Though I'm not sure what anyone there expected Jesus to do, there's no doubt that they did *not* expect Jesus to say the shocking thing he said: "Remove the stone" (John 11:39, NASB).

How could Jesus ask for such a thing? To tamper with the dead was unthinkable to the Jews. It was immoral. Broaching the awkwardness, Martha tried to explain, "Lord, by this time there will be a stench; for he has been dead four days" (11:39, NASB).

Jesus said to her, "Did I not say to you, if you believe, you will see the glory of God?" (11:40, NASB). Jesus spoke with such authority that the whole dynamic changed. As I envision the scene, every person there sensed the presence of a power that infused them with a willingness to cooperate. Spontaneously, the family and friends of

Lazarus self-organized. The men worked together to move the stone. Then Jesus began to pray, not a petition, but a word of thanksgiving: "Father, I thank You that You heard Me. And I knew that You hear Me always; but because of the people standing around I said it, that they may believe that You did send Me" (John 11:41b-42, NASB).

The doubt-free confidence expressed in Jesus' prayer convicted Mary and Martha. Both sisters saw the contrast between Jesus' faith and theirs. His faith in God was sure. Theirs wasn't.

No one in world history has ever trusted God as Jesus did. That's why the writer of Hebrews says that Jesus is "the Author and Perfecter of faith" (Hebrews 12:2, NASB).

- *Faith* is what enabled him to journey through Judea without being afraid of getting killed.
- *Faith* is what enabled him to know that Lazarus's sickness wasn't unto death.
- *Faith* is what empowered him to believe God heard his prayers.
- *Faith* is what gave him confidence to thank God in advance for raising Lazarus.
- And *faith* is what strengthened him to rage against death and unbelief, so that he could summon Lazarus from the dead.

With a loud voice, Jesus cried out, "Lazarus! Come forth!" (John 11:43). This was the triumph that Jesus had postponed—the triumph of resurrected life. I can just see Lazarus with streamers of burial wrappings dangling from his arms and legs. I believe the sight of him provided visual proof that Jesus' faith in God was realistic.

Faith in God *today* is realistic. Without it, we can't generate godly anger. Jesus could not have raged had he been wrestling with inner doubts and unexpressed complaints about God. Jesus is the author, not of doubt, but of faith. As the writer of Hebrews explains it, "Faith is the assurance of things hoped for, the conviction [literally, the convince-ment] of things not seen" (Hebrews 11:1).

Faith, not blind faith. Faith, not omniscient certainty. Faith—the thing we all have to have in order to please God. As I already mentioned before, the Bible says it unequivocally: "And without faith, it is impossible to please God" (Hebrews 11:6). Impossible.

Jesus was thus displeased by the faithlessness of those who were involved in Lazarus's funeral. By saying this, I'm not minimizing the notable faith of Martha, who faithfully confessed that Jesus is "the Christ, the Son of God." Nor am I discounting her belief in the future resurrection of God's people. Nor am I forgetting Martha's other faith-filled statement, "Even now, I know that whatever You ask of God, God will give You" (John 11:22, NASB). On the contrary, I'm declaring that Jesus' anger rages against death and unbelief. Because Jesus loves us—because he is a friend of sinners—he sees death and unbelief as enemies. Death is an enemy that steals life as we know it, and unbelief an enemy that steals people's faith in God.

How many of us today are like the weepers at Lazarus's tomb, who allowed death and unbelief to steal their faith? How many of us are living with a low view of God, expecting so little of God that we barely take time to pray? Do we, too, accuse God of depriving us? How many of us feel frustrated with Jesus' unwillingness to prevent certain tragedies from happening? How humbly do we trust in God's word?

If we don't *functionally* trust God's word, then we don't trust God's word. If we don't trust God's word, we don't trust God.

How can we trust God if we secretly believe that God doesn't have our back? Why should anyone take a chance, as Jesus did by traveling through Judea, where people were trying to kill him, if we think God is unreliable or nonexistent? Why go out of our way to vie for truthfulness in our relationships if God isn't going to be there to shield us when people shun us for refusing to accept blatant lies? Why help molested boys if our efforts are going to be scorned, not thanked? Why take any personal risk for the sake of pleasing God if God is merely a matter of religion, not real life?

I can see why Jesus raged. Jesus was infuriated by death and unbelief because both make people fall into despair. Both tempt Christians to retreat rather than rally. Both lure us into believing that doubts about God are practical and wise. Both trick us into living without faith. Both sucker us into functioning like atheists.

How many of us (perhaps secretly) have said something like one of these complaints?

- "Lord, if you had been here, the children would not have been sexually abused."
- "Lord, if you loved me, I wouldn't be sick."
- "Lord, if you were both all-powerful and all-loving, you never would've permitted this to happen."

See why Jesus raged? Inwardly he raged at the devilish imposition of death and unbelief for steering people away from basic truth. Inwardly he raged because the snake-like scales of doubt and fear of death cover people's eyes so they can't see. Jesus inwardly exploded because things could be so much better if you and I would take risks that exercise faith in God and display God's faithfulness before the eyes of unbelievers who are watching.

Every day, Christians should be confronting the problem of doubt and nurturing each other's faith in God. Are we confronting doubt or together caving to it?

"You can't fight city hall," says a roomful of scared Christians who doubt that God will help them make things right. When Hitler took over Germany, countless numbers of Christians chose to turn a blind eye to obscenities. "What if we get punished? What if we get fired? What if we lose our paychecks?" These are statements of unbelief made by Christians who feel intimidated and unwilling to voice their testimonies in public. "I'm with God," says someone totally unwilling to take a risk. "God is nice and neutral, and I am neutral, too. I just want to be nice to people and have people be nice to me."

Jesus snorted like a horse because he knew that God is faithful—despite what people say about God untruthfully. Jesus raged within himself for the sake of the glory of God. Indeed, he knew the power of God, and he knew the power of prayer, and he knew that God *does* listen, and he knew that taking action in God's timing with God's help can realistically lead to a public miracle.

Story 11: Jesus Reproached His Disciples

I am blown away by the high standards of our God. Though his standards are unattainable, they become attainable if only we will walk by faith. With God, it's faith or bust. Apart from faith, we cannot please God. God wants faith—active faith, not mere nods and mental assent. God requires more from us than generalized agreement that says, "Yeah, I believe all of that stuff." God's standards are so high that God expects us—commands us—to take seriously God's word and count on the fulfillment of God's promises. When we trust God, we find out that faith is dignifying. It exalts us to a higher plane of living. God honors us *just by asking us* to trust God. God gives us the opportunity to experience God's faithfulness in our own lives.

You'd think God might let up some, but God doesn't. God is holy. God's unchanging. God's unwilling to lower God's standards at our expense. God insists on calling us ever upward, even in the face of tragic deaths. Talk about anger lessons. Who else in the world but Jesus would chastise his disciples even while they were grieving his own death? Jesus was so faithful that he constantly lived up to God's high standards. What is even more remarkable to me is that Jesus pressed his disciples to join with him in living a higher way. Let's review the story of what happened.

After Jesus had been crucified and it was confirmed to Pilate that Jesus was dead, Jesus' body was carefully wrapped in linen, then laid in a tomb. According to the Gospel of Mark, on the third day after his death, early in the morning, three women came to the tomb to anoint his wrapped-up body with more spices. Just as they were wondering who might roll away the stone from the entrance of the tomb, they discovered that the stone had already been moved by someone else.

As they entered the tomb, they saw a young man in a white robe, who said to them, "You are looking for Jesus of Nazareth who was crucified. He has been raised. He is not here. . . . But go, tell his disciples and Peter, 'He is going before you to Galilee; there you will see him, just as he told you'" (Mark 16:6-7, NASB).

But instead, the women fled and told no one. They were too astonished. Too frozen. Too gripped. Too completely overwhelmed to say a word.

But then Jesus himself appeared to Mary Magdalene. When Mary Magdalene became an eyewitness of the resurrected Lord, she no longer kept silent. In fact, while the disciples were mourning and weeping in bereavement, she reported the news to them that Jesus had arisen from the dead. But Jesus' chosen disciples refused to believe it.

Sometime later, Jesus appeared in a different form to two men on the road to Emmaus. When those men, too, told the disciples that they had actually conversed with resurrected Jesus, the disciples once again did not believe it.

Let's ponder this for a moment. The apostles of Jesus Christ, hailed throughout church history, did not to believe the truth. Willfully, they dismissed the eyewitness testimonies of those who verified that Jesus had done exactly what he had preannounced he would do. Time and time again, he had told them in plain language that he would suffer, be killed, and on the third day rise again. Why did the apostles not expect his plain predictions to come true? The apostles even *wanted* his predictions to be true. But was it true? How could it be true?

These same eleven apostles had watched Jesus call forth Lazarus from the dead. But to summon back himself? To resurrect himself? How outlandish to believe that Jesus could actually nullify his own death! Jesus was dead. He had expired. He was gone. So the joke was on the followers of Jesus. They were the big suckers in this saga. Hook, line, and sinker—they had each fallen for it, the whole bit about him being the Messiah. So here they were now. The duped eleven. No way were they about to get sucked up into Jesus-wishes again. Been there, done that. Let others do the hallucinating. Leave the wishful thinking to the women. The disciples, doggone it, were grown men. They could handle this. They were fine. They just needed to be left alone.

So while the eleven were left alone in their man cave eating dinner, Jesus unexpectedly popped in. Just as lovingly and impolitely as ever, wouldn't you know the first thing Jesus did was to reproach them. Jesus reproached them at the dinner table. Despite all they had been through—seeing him suffer, watching him die, being tormented by their broken, shattered dreams. These disciples had been sleepless. I imagine that they had flashbacks and nightmares. They must have been so depleted. But Jesus still upheld God's same high standards. In their downward unbelief, Jesus called them upward once again.

Greeting them with a reprimand, he chided them for their pride and let them know that their hard-heartedness was utterly inexcusable. It didn't matter how tired they were. Exhaustion is no substitute for faith. Jesus asks for faith from all his followers. Over and over again, Jesus' anger points us to the same familiar refrain—that it's impossible to please God apart from faith. Faith is not an exercise in strenuously striving to be good enough for God. Faith is deep assurance in God's faithfulness. Jesus aimed his anger at the disciples' unbelief because it's the very thing that wearied them. A refusal to believe in God's great faithfulness is a refusal to take refuge in God's love.

God wants us to rest in God's great love. If we're too arrogant to rest, we'll be too haughty to believe, because we will be too tired to trust in Jesus.

So he reproached them. Mark's Gospel clearly tells the reason why: "He reproached them for their unbelief and hardness of heart" (Mark 16:14, NASB). What I'm saying is that Jesus reproached them for the purpose of unloading them. Jesus longed for his apostles to dump their unbelief. Yet so humble is our Lord that he demanded nothing more than just a tiny drop of faith from them.

How much faith does Jesus require from us today? I suppose just enough to motivate us to act as if God's promises are true. How much faith does a skydiver need? Just enough to jump out of the plane.

So when these same eleven apostles proceeded to Galilee to the mountain that Jesus had designated, they saw him, and they worshipped him. They worshipped, not with intellectual certainty, but rather with the giving of their lives. They gave themselves to Jesus, even though some still "doubted" (Matthew 28:17). They all jumped out of the plane, so to speak. Some skydived with worry, and some with jubilation. But all of them went free-falling through the air. All of them responded affirmatively to the instructions that he gave—which, by the way, ennobled them with purpose. Right after Jesus reproached them, this is what he said to the eleven: "All authority in heaven and on earth has been given to me. Go therefore and make disciples of all nations, baptizing them in the name of the Father and the Son and the Holy Spirit, teaching them to obey everything that I have commanded you; and remember, I am with you always, to the end of the age" (Matthew 28:18-20, NASB).

That's how it works in God's kingdom. We get reproached so we can be ennobled. We get relieved so we can find rest. It's a can't-lose situation for true followers of Christ. God loves us, so God disciplines us and scourges us with correction, so we might be partakers of God's holiness (Hebrews 12:5-10).

Chapter 7

How Does Jesus' Healing Anger Relate to Doubt?

My purpose in this chapter is to showcase the healing power of Jesus' anger, which flows to those who come to him in faith. What the following stories show is that the tiniest drop of faith—that is, the tiniest honest impulse to be truthful about God—makes all the difference with regard to pleasing Jesus. Those who are openly willing to submit to God's holy love experience Jesus' anger as a gift. But those who harden their hearts and doubt the living God encounter Jesus' anger in the form of censuring judgment that spotlights their unwillingness to repent.

Story 12: Jesus Rebuked a Demon in a Boy

Who can understand the mysterious interplay between sickness and demonic activity? I am not an expert on mental illness. But as a theologian, I believe Jesus' faith gave him miraculous healing power to exorcise a demon from a demon-possessed boy who was mentally ill. Let's review Matthew's version of the story:

And when they came to the multitude, a man came up to Him, falling on his knees before Him, saying, "Lord, have mercy on my son, for he is a lunatic, and is very ill; for he often falls into the fire, and often into the water. And I brought him to Your disciples, and they could not cure him." And Jesus answered and said, "O, unbelieving and perverted generation! How long shall I be with you? How long shall I put up with you? Bring him here to Me." And Jesus rebuked him, and the demon came out of him, and the boy was cured at once. Then the disciples came to Jesus privately and said, "Why could we not cast it out?" And He said to them, "Because of the littleness of your faith; for truly I say to you, if you have faith as a mustard seed, you shall say to this mountain, 'Move from here to there,' and it shall move; and nothing shall be impossible for you. But this kind does not go out except by prayer and fasting." (Matthew 17:14-21, NASB)

Jesus didn't suffer from littleness of faith. By faith, he rebuked this stubborn demon. By faith, Jesus prevailed. Faith fueled Jesus with courageous, loving anger that energized him and authorized him to drive this demon out. Jesus had faith at least four times over: he had the faith to pray, the faith to fast, the faith to have sinless anger, and the faith to use that anger to expel an extra-stubborn dark force.

Jesus' words to his disciples were faultfinding: "O unbelieving and perverted generation!" He didn't pad his honest thoughts with charming rhetoric. "How long shall I put up with you?" he said.

Was Jesus angry at his disciples for failing to cast out that demon? I don't know, but clearly he was not pleased. Yet Jesus loved them well in his displeasure. In my mind, Jesus' statement "How long should I put up with you?" reeks of exasperation. Still, Jesus served his followers nonetheless. Rather than resenting them or cynically giving up on them, he gave to them sacrificially.

Jesus understood that exposure was not enough to expel this demon. Exposure doesn't threaten any demon. Being *found* out is not the same as being *driven* out. Secrecy isn't the secret to a demon's tenacity. Being found out didn't matter, and it especially didn't matter when the disciples' faith turned out to be inadequate. Their sincerity of faith amounted to "littleness" of faith, according to Jesus. That demon didn't budge until Jesus approached it in anger. The biblical record shows that Jesus rebuked that demon by the power of pure trust in God. I like to say it this way: Jesus "faithed" that demon out.

If only the disciples had had more faith, Jesus said, they could have done far more. Given everything I have studied and observed, I believe that exorcisms can only be successful in the context of sacrificial love. Demons aren't responsive to shallow orders from the flesh. They know there's no authority in mere sincerity, and far less in pretension. Authority can't be feigned in the spiritual realm. In the social realm, of course, people believe all kinds of things. But demons don't have human gullibility. If a demon wants to nest in an infirm person, that demon is going to stay until required to move out.

Love is what forces demons out. Let me back up and say this a bit more carefully. Faith in the form of confidence and authority drives them out. Faith not in oneself, but in God's love. Faith animates a person to be angry to the point of exercising sacrificial love. Sacrificial anger—that's the kind of anger that brings healing.

Take note: Jesus didn't teach the demon—because demons are unteachable. Jesus *rebuked* the demon. To rebuke means to "beat back." Rebukes are commands. They're orders that tell another what to do. When Jesus calmed the storm, he said, "Hush!" When Jesus rebuked Peter, he said, "Get behind me!" When Jesus rebuked this particularly obstinate demon, he must have told the demon to come out.

When the disciples asked Jesus why they had failed to cast out the demon from this boy, Jesus answered frankly, "Because of the littleness of your faith."

Jesus could've said nothing more and ended the conversation. Instead, he gratuitously taught them. He tipped them in to the knowledge of what faith can actually do when faith is real. Just a tiny drop of faith, just a mustard seed of faith can move a mountain!

He said, "And nothing shall be impossible to you." Such is the nature of faith. When you have it, you understand that faith doesn't put its trust in the power of faith itself. Real faith trusts in God's power. Real faith is that stuff that hardly anybody has. Real faith trusts securely in God's character. Real faith understands that God is totally trustworthy even though God requires us to follow Jesus on a narrow path of suffering.

It is not coincidental that mere moments after Jesus cured the boy, Jesus said to his disciples, "The Son of Man is going to be delivered into the hands of men, and they will kill Him, and He will be raised up on the third day" (Matthew 17:22-23, NASB). Behold the triple faith of Jesus Christ: Jesus had faith to rebuke the demon, faith to rest assured that his not-so-impressive disciples could move a mountain by faith themselves, and faith to trust in God even though God had planned for Jesus to be delivered into the hands of murderers.

No wonder you and I have lacked the power to exorcise demons and heal afflicted boys. No wonder we haven't made a mountain move. Our problem, I believe, is that we haven't had self-sacrificial anger. Unlike Jesus, we haven't been willing to surrender ourselves enough to stand up in godly anger against evil. We typically don't care enough to suffer personal loss for the sake of God. Why is it so rare for us to fast from food together spiritually? Why is it abnormal for most professing Christians to be willing to endure persecution?

Because Jesus was willing to suffer for the sake of obeying God, he alone had the power of anger to cast that demon out. How much power do you and I have in Christ that we don't access for fear of suffering? Jesus did not fear suffering because Jesus did not fear evil. He wasn't afraid of evil because he was convinced that God is far greater than any evil. Jesus' fear of God made Jesus so fearless that he accessed the authority of holy anger.

What Irked the Pharisees

Jesus had spectacular power. None of the other religious leaders could do what Jesus did. They couldn't perform unprecedented miracles. They didn't know how to lead with right motives. They couldn't mesmerize a crowd. They couldn't manage a single day without seeking the approval of each other. They simply couldn't harness their insecurities. Consequently, there was nothing more annoying to these religious leaders than Jesus of Nazareth, the independent rabbi who took his cues from God.

What irked the Pharisees most about Jesus' use of power was that it never seemed to benefit *them*. Particularly with regard to Jesus' healing ministry, Jesus was so radically unselfish. You see, the problem is there was nothing for the Pharisees to exploit. There was no money from Jesus' healings to be stolen, no medical research to be seized, and no way to co-opt Jesus into their system. As a result, their strategy was to watch him vigilantly and see if they could trap him or accuse him.

Story 13: Jesus Was Angry with the Pharisees in the Synagogue

Next comes my rendition of the story of Jesus' anger in the synagogue. I have embellished it, as you will soon see. My aim is to explain why I think Jesus' anger is so beautiful.

One day when Jesus entered the synagogue, a man was there with a withered hand. The Pharisees were there, too, watching Jesus. Stealthily they watched with predatory eyes to see if Jesus would work a healing on the Sabbath.

For the man with the withered hand, this moment was unbelievable. Here he was with all these people, yet no one was staring at him. To him, it felt surreal to blend in. You see, his hand, all withered, looked like a strange sea creature. It was freakish, grotesque, seemingly subhuman. His hand was so offensive that it reliably repulsed practically everyone who saw it. All his life, this man had felt as though his hand was a traveling circus that commanded center stage in every room. But in this room, someone else took center stage. No doubt, the religious leaders realized that "that hand" was in the room. But they weren't staring at it disgustedly as usual. They were cautiously studying Jesus—which was exactly what made this moment unbelievable for this man.

Jesus said to him, "Rise and come forward!" (Mark 3:3, NASB).

With unhesitating obedience, the man with the withered hand stepped forward. That is, in stark vulnerability, he willingly joined Jesus on center stage. Expecting to feel demeaned by the audience of Pharisees, to his extreme surprise, he felt safe and dignified. Standing next to Jesus, he no longer felt ridiculous. On the contrary, he noticed that for the first time in his life, he felt like a normal person—as if his hand were somehow camouflaged by Jesus.

Then Jesus said to the Pharisees, "Is it lawful on the Sabbath to do good or to do harm, to save a life or to kill?" (Mark 3:4, NASB).

The Pharisees kept silent. So Jesus spoke again: "What person shall there be among you, who shall have one sheep, and if it falls into a pit on the Sabbath, will he not take hold of it, and lift it out? Of how much more value then is a person than a sheep? So then, it is lawful to do good on the Sabbath" (Matthew 12:11-12, NASB).

End of speech. End of teaching time. What need was there for any additional dialogue? The appointed time had come for Jesus to heal a person on the Sabbath, and no one among the Pharisees could stop him.

In the face of such depravity, Jesus looked around at them "with anger" (*met' orges*), "grieved" at their hardness of heart (Mark 3:5). How could they be so unfeeling? A man's whole life had been shaped by the shame of a deformity, yet the Pharisees didn't even care. They had no sensitivity, no ability whatsoever to empathize with another person's pain. They had dehumanized themselves.

Interestingly, the gospel writer Matthew uses the Greek word *anthropos* (which means "person, human being") to tell this story by calling the "man" with the withered hand an *anthropos* and saying that Jesus asked the Pharisees what *anthropos*—what human being—would not rescue a sheep if it fell. Matthew continues to make his point by saying that Jesus rhetorically asked the Pharisees, "Of how much more value is an *anthropos* [a person] than a sheep?"

All that is to say it was not inconsequential to Jesus—not something to be overlooked or minimized or excused—to see religious leaders so hardened that they couldn't feel compassion for a handicapped man. On account of their imagined superiority, they were impeded from regarding this dear *anthropos* not only as another human being, but as a *fellow* human being, someone just like them who was created in God's image just as they were.

Jesus said to the *anthropos*, his fellow human being, "Stretch out your hand!" (Mark 3:5).

Let me try to say it a little differently. Jesus, feeling angered by the Pharisees' attitudes and grieved at their hardness of heart, acted out his anger by healing a man in the synagogue on the Sabbath. In anger, Jesus acted. He acted in defiance, but *not* in defiance of the Pharisees' scorn for him personally. He acted rather in defiance of their legalism that rendered them compassionless. Angered by their heartlessness, he acted for the sake of a man for whom the Pharisees felt nothing.

Since Jesus acted on the Sabbath day, the Jewish day of rest, the Pharisees decided that Jesus acted in defiance of the law. On account of what they perceived to be Jesus' lawlessness, subjectively they judged him to be renegade. In their faithlessness toward God, they considered Jesus insubordinate.

Unconscious of their own extreme hypocrisy, the Pharisees relished this moment. They saw it as providing hard evidence to use against Jesus in court. From the Pharisees' warped perspective, Jesus didn't have it in him to follow their understanding of the law. He simply could not conform to their tradition. Thus, they in their pompousness were morbidly appalled by his open inattention to their misguided religiosity.

As they saw it, the hard evidence of Jesus' defiance was packaged in four words: "Stretch out your hand!" That statement, that performance, that miracle worked by Jesus was *worked* on the Sabbath day of rest. Jesus "worked" on the day of rest! To them it was clear that Jesus had broken the law in flagrant disregard of authority.

So when the man with the withered hand stretched out his hand, no one among the Pharisees marveled that it was instantly restored. No one gasped to see no scar. No one wondered to see no skin graft. No one clapped. No one cheered. No one's eyes flooded up with tears.

Sinful anger made the Pharisees blind. They couldn't see the beauty of the miracle. I don't think the Pharisees had even the slightest notion that they had handicapped themselves by pouring envy on the eyes of their own hearts. Inwardly blinded by envious rage, the Pharisees couldn't see their own unreasonableness in thinking that the Sabbath was a day to rest from righteousness and love. Fooled by their own folly, the Pharisees turned the Sabbath into a recess time for lawless self-indulgence.

The gospel writer Mark says the Pharisees then went out—on the Sabbath—and began taking counsel with certain political leaders, the Herodians, who supported King Herod, as to how they might together destroy Jesus (Mark 3:6). Because the Pharisees were sinning, they couldn't see that they were *working* on the Sabbath. Their hypocrisy was so thick that they were not even embarrassed by the irony.

When the hypocrites departed, I believe Jesus beamed at his new friend. I can just imagine Jesus shaking his friend's new hand in celebration. I can also see him doing a first-century high five. As for the man with the healed hand, I envisage him applauding, giving Jesus a big hand. Jesus risked his life for this man's healing.

In part, Jesus was angry at the Pharisees because in violating this man, they were violating themselves. I am personally convinced that Jesus entered the synagogue on that special day not only to heal the man with the strange sea-creature-like hand, but also to attempt to heal the Pharisees. But the Pharisees *didn't want* to be healed.

Did Jesus hold a grudge against the Pharisees for this? No, on the contrary, the Pharisees held a grudge against him. They begrudged Jesus for showing them God's ways. They hated this extraordinary rabbi. They hated him for exposing their inhumanity. Yet they failed to understand that his purpose was not to embarrass them arbitrarily or to shame them with a one-up power play. His purpose was to heal them—to rehumanize their hearts. But they did not desire to be rehumanized. In their hardened state of mind, they wanted to be higher than humanity. They wanted to be higher than that *anthropos* who was healed of his unseemly withered hand. The Pharisees, in fact, wanted to be higher than Jesus. That was the Pharisees' sin. They envied God-in-the-Flesh because they wanted to be God themselves.

So while they went out to plot Jesus' undoing, he went out to a mountain to stay up all night in prayer (Luke 6:11-12). I believe Jesus spent hours praying with compassion for each one of them.

Story 14: Jesus Raged When He Healed a Leper

Perhaps the most perplexing story of Jesus' anger is found in Mark 1:40-45. In this peculiar episode, a leper came to Jesus, fell on his knees, and said, "If you are willing, you can make me clean" (Mark 1:40). Not surprisingly, Jesus said he was willing. But astonishingly for that culture, Jesus reached out and touched the leper. According to the Mosaic law, physically touching a leper defiles a person.

There is so much theology to unpack here. First of all, Jesus cared more about the condition of the leper than his own religious standing in the community. Jesus took a social risk of becoming ceremonially unclean, which means he risked being made a social outcast. Not only did Jesus risk contracting leprosy, he also risked becoming sinful when he, the Son of God, emptied himself of his equality with God, put on human flesh, and dwelt in close proximity with sinners (Philippians 2:6-7).

Have you noticed how contagious sin is? It is harder *not* to sin when you hang around with people who are sinning willfully. The apostle Paul put it this way: "Do not be deceived: bad company corrupts good morals" (1 Corinthians 15:33, NASB).

Jesus kept his good morals. He was tempted in every way—to show off, to feel sorry for himself, to indulge in illicit pleasure, to be impatient, to be self-righteous, to abuse his messianic power, to mistreat people, to disobey God, to doubt the perfect love of God the Father. Yet Jesus faithfully upheld God's standards of righteousness, not only in his actions, but also in the privacy of his heart.

Jesus, fully human, stayed immune to leprosy, just as Jesus stayed immune to sin itself. Somehow the "bad company" of the sinners all around him did not corrupt Jesus in his humanity. I believe the way that Jesus stayed pure was by being fully truthful in his heart. Jesus judged every sin as being sinful. He was never callous or cavalier about any violation of God's law.

So when Jesus reached out and touched the leper who was kneeling before him, asking to be healed, the leper, indeed, was healed. Instead of Jesus catching leprosy, the leper caught Jesus' good health. The Bible says, "Immediately the leprosy left him, and he was made clean" (Mark 1:42, NASB).

Now comes the peculiar part of this revealing story. Jesus was angry when he healed that leper, and Jesus raged as he sent the leper away. Question: Why was Jesus angry? And, by the way, how are we to *know* that Jesus was angry? Most English translations of the Greek New Testament omit the two Greek words that signal to us the presence of Jesus' anger.

Let me try to make this clear. The New American Standard Bible in English says this: "And moved with compassion, He stretched out his hand, and touched him, and said to him, 'I am willing; be cleansed.' And immediately the leprosy left him and he was cleansed. And He sternly warned him and immediately sent him away" (Mark 1:41-43). But the ancient Greek manuscripts say two different things where the translators have written "moved with compassion": some of them say *splanchnistheis* (in English, "moved to compassion"), and others say *orgistheis* (in English, "being angry"). Since something has to account for this discrepancy, our job is to figure out what that is. In other words, we have to find a reason to explain why some manuscripts say *splanchnistheis* and some say *orgistheis.*

It is important to understand that a basic rule in translating ancient texts is to assume the more difficult reading is the true one. Since it is harder to explain why Jesus was angry, I believe Jesus was angry. In other words, I believe the reason why the word *orgistheis* appears in ancient manuscripts is that it was the original word Mark used. To say the same thing differently, it is easier to presume that ancient scribes changed the word *orgistheis* to *splanchnistheis* than vice versa. I believe Christian scribes edited out Jesus' anger for PR reasons. Given the Stoic influence back then (which counted all anger as bad), I believe the reason why *splanchnistheis* ("moved to compassion") appears in some ancient manuscripts is that editorial scribes altered the original Greek to make it look more respectable in a society that was influenced by Stoic bias.

Here is what I believe the original text says: Jesus, "being angry . . . stretched out His hand, and touched him [the leper], and said to him,

'I am willing; be cleansed'" (Mark 1:41). This rendering accords with the interesting fact that the Greek word *embrimaomai* shows up in this passage as well. As you may recall from chapter 6, *embrimaomai* literally means "to snort like a horse." It means "to rage." What we find in Mark 1:43 is that Jesus, for some reason, snorted like a horse (*embrimasamenos*). Yet he raged in such a way that the leper didn't even seem to notice.

I believe that in this instance, Jesus' anger was similar to what it was at the tomb of Lazarus. Jesus loved this leper. Jesus *healed* this leper. Jesus went so far as to touch the leper physically, as if to welcome that untouched leper back into community. How long had it been since the leper had been touched by anyone? Lepers don't get touched. They don't get hugged. I'm trying to imagine how I would feel after years and years of being cut off from all physical affection. When Jesus touched the leper, I believe, Jesus healed his emotional woundedness, not just leprosy.

Jesus' anger, as I see it, was purifying. Just as Jesus was offended by the fever that afflicted Peter's mother-in-law, so Jesus was enraged by the leprosy that infected this dear leper. I think it is telling that Mark's Gospel says that when Jesus told the leper to be cleansed, "immediately the leprosy left him, and he was made clean" (Mark 1:42). The Bible says the leprosy "left" him. The leprosy departed. I wonder if it fled. To me, it sounds like that leprosy vanished in response to Jesus' authority just as demons hightailed it at the sound of Jesus' command.

Then Jesus raged. Where the New American Standard Version says, "sternly warned," the Greek says *embrimasamenos*. I believe what happened is that Jesus' anger burned for the leper's sake. After cleansing out the leprosy, Jesus sent the leper away with these special parting words: "See that you say nothing to anyone; but go, show yourself to the priest and offer for your cleansing what Moses commanded, for a testimony to them" (Mark 1:44, NASB).

Jesus' instructions to the leper were echoes from Leviticus 13. There the law provides instructions for dealing ceremonially with leprosy. The law requires lepers to show themselves to the priest so that the priest can diagnose the situation. The priest's job was to *look at* the leper, not touch the leper. Yet Jesus, the priest of priests, had physically touched the leper and miraculously healed him.

How did the healed man respond? Not with gratitude, as many have suggested. This man wasn't humbly overjoyed. Had that been the case, then Jesus wouldn't have raged. To think the healed man was overflowing with uncontainable joy is to assume that Jesus was moved with compassion, yet the Greek says Jesus raged.

Why would Jesus rage? I believe he raged because this healed leper responded to Jesus' gift with flagrant disobedience at every level. First of all, he did *not* keep the matter confidential but instead went out and broadcast it. Second, he did *not* go show himself to the priest. Third, he did *not* "offer what Moses commanded" (which was to offer sacrifices spelled out in Leviticus 14). The Bible doesn't describe in detail all that this man did except to say that he "went out and began to proclaim it freely and to spread the news about, to such an extent that Jesus could no longer publicly enter a city, but stayed out in unpopulated areas" (Mark 1:45, NASB). My hunch, however, is that he went out, swaggering, and bragged.

To brag about Jesus' gift is to objectify the gift instead of personalizing the gift and understanding it as a pronouncement of God's love. I don't think this man whom Jesus physically touched ever understood that Jesus loved him. I think he was like the Pharisees who simply wanted glory for themselves. Therefore, this empty man missed out on the deepest healing Jesus offered him.

I am glad that Jesus was angry. I love it that Jesus hates it when people mistake God's grace for a badge of their own honor and acclaim. What mattered was the *man,* yet this formerly leprous man stayed way too self-absorbed to find that out. Despite Jesus' grace and Jesus' protective rage, this touched-by-Jesus man remained untouched—and thus unhealed—in his deepest pain. I believe that explains why this healed man was disobedient, even though Jesus graced him with a miracle.

Story 15: Jesus Reproached Three Cities

This last story of Jesus' anger in the Gospels occurred after three whole cities of people responded to his miracles with nothing but sighing yawns of faithlessness.

The Bible says Jesus "reproached" the cities where most of his miracles were done. To reproach means to express disapproval or anger about something. English synonyms for reproach include blame, chide, reprimand, and upbraid. The Greek word for reproach in the New Testament is *oneidizo*. The word *oneidizo* appears in Jesus' Sermon on the Mount when he says, "Blessed are you when people reproach [*oneidizein*] you and persecute you and say all kinds of evil against you falsely, on account of Me" (Matthew 5:11, NASB).

Jesus reproached whole cities. Matthew names three cities that Jesus reproached: Bethsaida, Chorazin, and Capernaum. He reproached them because they bore witness to Jesus' miracles yet did not repent. Here's what Jesus said to them explicitly:

> Woe to you, Chorazin! Woe to you, Bethsaida! For if the miracles had occurred in Tyre and Sidon which occurred in you, they would have repented long ago in sackcloth and ashes. Nevertheless I say to you, it will be more tolerable for Tyre and Sidon in the day of judgment than for you. And you, Capernaum, will not be exalted to heaven, will you? You will descend to Hades; for if the miracles had occurred in Sodom which occurred in you, it would have remained to this day. (Matthew 11:21-23, NASB)

When Jesus told these cities to repent, he didn't burden them with a list of dos and don'ts to help them alter their behavior. Nor did he assign them any penance. Nor did he pressure them. Jesus knew they had no power to self-redeem. None of us can manage to correct our character flaws with our own willpower. When Jesus called for repentance, he didn't load people up; on the contrary, he attempted to *unload* them. Look at what he said to these three cities: "Come to Me, all who are weary-laden, and I will give you rest. Take My yoke upon you, and learn from Me; for I am gentle and humble in heart; and you shall find rest for your souls. For My yoke is easy, and My load is light" (Matthew 11:28-30, NASB).

To repent means to surrender to the truth. It means to come clean with regard to the truth of who we are and what we've done. It means to stop making excuses. It means to care enough to change from the inside out. True repentance has to do with internal change. The Greek word *metanoia* literally means an afterthought (*meta,* meaning "after" and *noia,* meaning "thought"), a changing of the mind. As Dallas Willard used to say, to repent is to "rethink your thinking." Right thinking yields right feeling. Right thoughts produce right emotions. A truthful mind subjected to God gives way to a right perspective.

Deep down, we all know that we need to adjust ourselves. To repent means to adjust *internally* so that we are not the same *externally.* Repentance starts and ends with being truthful with ourselves.

What I have found from following Jesus for nearly fifty years is that the more we tell the truth, the more God lightens our load. In my twenties and early thirties, I carried a heavy load that I didn't even know was heavy until after I had put it down. It was not a load of anger; it was a load of selfish fear. I was so fearful. Scared about my looks, scared I would never get married, scared that I would somehow miss out. I had so much fear that it distracted me from noticing my anger.

But as I have said before, I really didn't *want* to see my anger. Perhaps my biggest problem was that I didn't want my problem to be my problem. Lots of Christians have that problem. Who wants to be a Christian who has anger deep inside but is way too scared to admit that to anyone else? Given the strains of Stoicism that stream through Christian circles and mislead us into thinking anger is always bad, there seem to be countless Christians who, just like myself, were never taught to engage their own honest feelings. How do people *find* their own feelings?

For me, the starting point was to address my eating patterns. For others, the starting point might be to look at their sexual sins, or procrastination patterns, or slothfulness in not taking care of something. Another starting point is to address the part of your life that you *least* want to address. When I found my taboo subject—which was my Christian parents' divorce and my unaddressed feelings about what had happened—I slowly began to realize I was angry. I discovered that my fear load was not my only load. I also had an anger load that warded me away from finding my raw sadness.

I believe the people of Bethsaida, Chorazin, and Capernaum were sinners like me who didn't want to face their raw pain. They didn't want to feel it, so they hid it from themselves by loading it upon their own backs. The people in these cities were too prideful to expose their vulnerability, so they lied to themselves by denying their vulnerability. Then their dishonesty blinded them. Due to their spiritual blindness, they could not see what Jesus' miracles revealed about Jesus.

Tragically, these three cities refused to understand that God is greater than the tragedies in our lives. God is greater than our sins. God is greater than our pain. God is greater than our most devastating losses. The people in these cities were not able to apprehend the reality of God's greatness because they were flat-out unwilling to be amazed.

Un-amazed people are smug. Smugness produces questions such as this: "What's the big deal if Jesus can work a miracle but I am still in want for something more?" I believe the people in these unbelieving cities wanted something other than dazzling miracles of healing and redemption. They wanted money. They wanted pleasure. They wanted national superiority and power. In their minds, Jesus was something less than a real messiah. To them, Jesus was a great big disappointment.

How encouraged should people be by Jesus' miracles? What are we to make of the historical fact that Jesus healed the sick and blind and lame, and calmed the storm, and stilled the sea, and raised Lazarus from the grave? The people in these cities weren't encouraged by the fact that Jesus gave observable proof (in his astounding miracles) that anything is possible with God.

With God, there is always hope—real hope, not wishful thinking. Hope is not idealism. It is not naive. It's more powerful than that. Hope derives directly from proven character, and proven character from perseverance, and perseverance from tribulation. The apostle Paul explains this in the context of his letter to the Romans: "And we exult in hope of the glory of God. And not only this, but we also exult in our tribulations, knowing that tribulation brings about perseverance, and perseverance proven character, and proven character, hope, and hope does not disappoint, because the love of God has been poured within our hearts through the Holy Spirit who was given to us" (Romans 5:2b-5, NASB). Hope is such a wonder because, despite its clear acknowledgment of every person's sinfulness and all creation's brokenness, it still doggedly hopes. Hope hopes to the point of enabling us to *exult* in our tribulations.

To exult (*kauchometha*) means "to rejoice, to celebrate." In Christ, it is realistic to delight in our tribulations because we know that God is using them to transform us. This different kind of hope—this godly biblical hope—hopes against all hope because real hope hopes *in God* (Romans 4:18).

The problem, I believe, with the people of Bethsaida, Chorazin, and Capernaum was that they accused Jesus of depriving them. Once they saw he was a miracle worker, I believe, they decided they were personally deserving of a lot more than what he had given them. To them, Jesus' miracles were annoyingly incomplete. If Jesus was the Messiah, then why didn't he remove all pain? If Jesus was the long-awaited Savior, then why didn't he save people from the insult and embarrassment of having to repent from sin? The people in these cities didn't want to have to repent. They weren't interested in repentance or transformation. They were interested in themselves, not God.

No wonder Jesus reproached them.

He scolded them, whole cities, because they rejected the good gifts of faith and hope. I believe faith and hope seem very unattractive to people who have neither. The people in these cities had neither. These people didn't want to have faith. Faith acts. These people didn't want to take action. How humbling is it to take action in obedience to God? Faith agrees to do what God wants. Having faith means deferring to God's wisdom. Taking steps of faith means stepping out in love, not selfishness. It means doing what is right instead of taking the easy way out.

The people in these cities, as I imagine them, preferred an easy way out. They were focused on the concrete here and now. They didn't have time to hope. Hope waits.

When people refuse to wait on the living God, eventually they become hopeless. Hopelessness makes people exploitative. It turns them inward, making them desperate—so desperate that they'll lie to get what they want. When Jesus reproached the citizens of Chorazin, Bethsaida, and Capernaum, he reproached their hopelessness. He didn't personally shun them in anger; he renounced their sin in anger. Then he invited them, as persons, to himself.

"Come to me," he said.

Jesus basically said the same thing to his apostles. Three of his apostles were hometown boys of two of these three reprimanded cities.

"Follow me," he said to Peter and Andrew of Bethsaida (Matthew 4:19).

"Follow me," he said to Philip, who was likewise from Bethsaida (John 1:43).

"Follow me," he said to Matthew, a tax gatherer from Capernaum (Matthew 9:9).

"Come to me," Jesus says to us today. If we'll go to him, he will give us life-giving faith and life-giving hope that cannot disappoint. Hope gives people rest, even in our pain and tribulations. We can rest when we are hopeful because hope points us away to something greater than ourselves. Hope turns our attention to God.

But...

But what if we are angry at God? Was Jesus ever angry at God? That's what the next chapter is about.

Chapter 8

Was Jesus Ever Angry at God the Father?

None of the gospel writers report of anyone ever praising Jesus' humility. People marveled at his love. They gasped at his miracles. They expressed amazement at his wisdom. They were taken aback by his audacity. But no one ever said, "I can't believe how humble Jesus is." Even when he removed his outer garment, lowered himself, and washed his disciples' feet, the record does not indicate that anybody lauded his humility. Was Jesus too intimidating to be called humble? Or were those around him just too prideful to acknowledge it?

Humility is often misunderstood. Many seem to think that humility holds people back by causing them to say, "Who am I to challenge people? Who am I to take the lead? Who am I to point out something that is wrong?" Humility is mistaken for self-doubt.

True humility, I believe, is a dignifying attribute that strengthens the human spirit and tightens the inner fibers of the soul. Humility tethers people to reality. It makes them earthy, not platitudinous; secure, not insecure. Humility hitches people to the truth.

Truth strengthens people, and pride weakens people. Pride shrinks our capacity for the truth. Pride is thus intrinsically dishonest.

It takes humility to accept the truth as truth. That is why most people prefer to be lied to. It's why people shun the prophets and tune out the still, small voice. Who can hear the truth of their own sin? Who has the capacity to stomach the real truth about the dark side of their parents and children? Who is willing to look squarely at the evil people promote by refusing to be truthful about it?

Jesus was consistently truthful. In fact, he was resented for his perfect truthfulness. "But because I speak the truth," he said, "you do not believe me" (John 8:45, NASB). In the very next breath, he added, "If I speak truth, why do you not believe me?" (8:46).

The apostle Paul echoed the same refrain: "Have I now become your enemy by telling you the truth?" Paul asked (Galatians 4:16, NASB). Truth is just too hard for pride to swallow.

The rock-hard, diamond-like, solid, simple truth is that God is entirely faithful. Why, then, do we doubt God? Why does anyone wonder if God is real? Because of our frustrations and disappointments? Because of injustice? Because of the awful things that happen to other people? We don't trust God because of that? When did God ever tell us that life on earth would be painless? God has faithfully told us just the opposite. God said if Adam and Eve were to eat the forbidden fruit, they would die. After they disobeyed God and ate the forbidden fruit, God told them that the measure of their pain would be multiplied exponentially (Genesis 3:14-19). Shall we doubt God for being honest about that?

The truth, according to Jesus, is that we will have tribulation in this world (John 16:33). But just as true as that—and even truer still, since this is eternal—is the truth that he has overcome the world (John 16:33). Pain does not disprove God's faithfulness. It actually provides a backdrop for displaying the awesome victory of his faithfulness. God is greater than the evils that invade us. God is greater than our protests, greater than our doubts, and greater than our maddening cries of "Why?":

- "Why is this happening to me?"
- "Why are people subjected to such hideous, obscene things?"
- "Why, why, why does God allow this?"

The spoken word *why* in Aramaic sounds like a bleating lamb. It's *lama*, pronounced "laah maah" like a sheep's sound, "baa, baa." The word itself bleats and bleeds. So Jesus cried on the cross, "My God, my God! Why [*Lama*] hast Thou forsaken Me?" (Matthew 27:47, NASB). Jesus Christ, the Lamb of God, bleated on the cross as he bled.

Jesus experienced trauma. He knows what it feels like to be crushed. He knows what it is like to be abandoned, invaded, disrespected, betrayed, and abused. He even knows what it's like to be subjected to a rigged mock trial, to be lied about in court, to be framed.

Jesus, the Man of Sorrows, knows the agony of crying out, "Why?" He viscerally endured the thick darkness and confusion of unrelenting anguish that didn't let up until he died. He exemplified for us that it is *not a sin* to be overwhelmed.

"Why?" is a valid cry for an overwhelmed human being overflooded by harsh torrents of desperation. In this context, "Why?" is not a question of curiosity. The question "Why?" has nothing to do with intellectual inquiries when it is whimpered or wailed by a hurting, howling desecrated soul. *Why?* is a word of raw pain.

Job's Cry "Why?"

When Job in the Old Testament was struck by a series of back-to-back calamities from Satan, he responded in humility with worship. "The Lord gave, and the Lord has taken away," he said. "Blessed be the Name of the Lord" (Job 1:21, NASB).

Instead of harboring resentment or bailing out on God, Job accepted the severity of his losses. He lost his livestock (all his herds of oxen, sheep, donkeys, and camels), all but three of his servants, and all of his daughters and sons. Even so, Job didn't fight against God. Job declined the opportunity to blame the living God. The Bible says that Job did not sin (1:22).

But then Satan smote Job with sore boils. From the sole of his foot to the crown of his head, Job was blanketed with pus-producing boils. So Job took a potsherd to scrape his crusty sores and sat among the ashes in misery.

Then Job's wife said to him, "Do you still hold fast your integrity? Curse God and die!" (2:9). Still Job maintained his integrity. He said to his wife, "You speak as one of the foolish women speaks. Shall we indeed accept good from God and not accept adversity?" (2:10).

Job's comment to his wife might seem culturally insensitive today. It might sound snippy and judgmental or chauvinistic. But the Bible says that in saying this, Job did *not* sin with his lips (2:10). Up to this point, Job's humility prevailed. His humility enabled him to be truthful. Job's humble mind-set prevented him from saying something vain and histrionic such as, "Who am I to tell my wife that her input is unhelpful? Who am I to direct attention to the foolish way she is speaking?"

Humility harnesses people. It reins in fleshly impulses. But humility, at the same time, isn't stifling. Humility doesn't lessen a person's confidence or resolve. It doesn't make people feel reticent to do what God says is right. Nor does it hold them back (after being slow to speak) from being outspoken. Humility does the opposite. It *increases* people's confidence and prompts them to do the right thing. Humility frees people by grounding them in truth. It liberates them from pride that would cause them otherwise to be dishonest and self-serving and afraid.

Job let his humility slip away. After seven days and nights of grueling silence with his three friends and no relief and no real comfort despite

their presence and their effort to attend him, Job's humble faith began
to wane. Because his agony persisted, he broke the weeklong silence
and jettisoned his humility overboard. Job became presumptuous and
cursed the day of his birth. Feeling justified in his anger, he said:

> Let the day perish on which I was to be born,
> and the night which said, "A boy is conceived."
> May that day be darkness;
> Let not God above care for it, nor light shine on it.
> Let darkness and black gloom claim it;
> Let a cloud settle on it;
> Let the blackness of the day terrify it.
>
> As for that night, let darkness seize it;
> Let it not rejoice among the days of the year;
> Let it not come into the number of months.
> Behold, let that night be barren;
> Let no joyful shout enter it.
> Let those curse it who curse the day . . .
> Because it did not shut the opening of my mother's womb or
> hide trouble from my eyes.
> (Job 3:3-10, NASB)

Job couldn't take it. His complaint was that his suffering was too
much. He felt vexed by what he deemed to be unbearable. If you read
aloud his diatribe (3:11-23) you might audibly hear his pain:

Why [*lama*] did I not die at birth? (v. 11a)

Why [*lama*] did the knees receive me? (v. 12a)

Why [*lama*] the breasts, that I should suck? (v. 12b)

Why [*lama*] is light given to him who suffers? (v. 20a)

Why [*lama*] is light given to a man whose way is hidden,
and whom God has hedged in? (v. 23)

Job thought he knew better than God. According to Job's lament, had he, Job, not been suckled, he would have been discarded like a miscarriage. Had he died as a newborn babe, he would have lain down in death and been quiet (3:13, 16). But Job did *not* die. Providentially, instead, he was swallowed up in pain. Wretchedly, he pronounced this thrashing, selfish claim: "I am not at ease. Nor am I quiet. And I am not at rest, but turmoil comes" (3:26).

It is difficult to admit that Job's anger was selfish. How could God expect him to be stable in his faith when Satan was wreaking such havoc in Job's life? I realize many Christians want to justify Job's anger, but I believe the Scriptures make it evident, as we shall see, that his anger was fueled by something other than faith.

Job knew that his anger was ungodly. So Job repented in dust and ashes. But Job did not repent until the end of the book of Job (chapter 42), yet God restored Job's fortune nonetheless.

Jeremiah's Cry "Why?"

The prophet Jeremiah anguished, too. Unlike Job, who was tormented directly by Satan, Jeremiah was attacked by corrupt religious leaders who schemed against him. These religious leaders deliberately devised and premeditated evil to punish Jeremiah for speaking the truth to them. Truth was intolerable to their ears. So they ambushed Jeremiah and punished him so brutally that he launched into the following harangue:

Look and see if there is any pain like my pain
Which was severely dealt out to me,
Which the Lord inflicted on the day of His fierce anger.
From on high He sent fire into my bones,

And it prevailed over them.

He has spread a net for my feet.

He has turned me back;

He has made me desolate;

Faint all day long. (Lamentations 1:12-13, NASB)

I am the man who has seen affliction. . . .

Even when I cry out and call for help, He [God] shuts out
      my prayer . . .

He [God] has made my paths crooked, . . .

He has turned aside my ways and torn me to pieces; . . .

He has made me desolate.

He bent His bow

And set me as a target for the arrow.

He made the arrows of His quiver

To enter into my inward parts.

I have become a laughingstock to all my people,

Their mocking song all the day.

He has filled me with bitterness,

He has made me drunk with wormwood.

And He has broken my teeth with gravel;

He has made me cower in the dust.

And my soul has been rejected from peace;

I have forgotten happiness. (Lamentations 3:1-17, NASB)

Jeremiah was the weeping prophet, Judah's scapegoat. When Pashhur the priest heard Jeremiah prophesying about dreadful, horrible things regarding God's judgment on God's people, Pashhur had Jeremiah physically beaten. Pashhur the priest! The chief officer in the house of the Lord had Jeremiah beaten for telling the truth. Jeremiah, bruised and broken, was then clamped into the stocks—regarded as a criminal.

Aghast at the unfairness of it all, Jeremiah cast the blame on God:

O Lord, Thou hast deceived me, and I was deceived;
Thou hast overcome me and prevailed.
I have become a laughingstock all day long;
Everyone mocks me.
For each time I speak, I cry aloud;
I proclaim violence and destruction
Because for me the word of the Lord has resulted
In reproach and derision all day long.
(Jeremiah 20:7-8, NASB)

Like Job, Jeremiah couldn't bear the brunt of tribulation. He couldn't take it without ventilating anger. Gasping for air as if choking on affliction, Jeremiah somehow managed, after spewing his resentment, to remember the real truth of God's good character. Heaving himself up, he revised his complaint by turning his jeremiad into worship:

But the Lord is with me like a dread champion;
Therefore my persecutors will stumble and not prevail.
They will be utterly ashamed, because they have failed,
With an everlasting disgrace that will not be forgotten.
Yet, O Lord of hosts, Thou who dost test the righteous,
Who sees the mind and the heart;
Let me see Thy vengeance on them;
For to Thee I have set forth my cause.
Sing to the Lord, praise the Lord!
For He has delivered the soul of the needy one
From the hand of evildoers. (Jeremiah 20:11-13, NASB)

But then he sank once again after that. Bobbing up and down, almost drowning in desperation, Jeremiah went from praise to remonstrance yet again. Seized by the anger of self-righteousness and self-pity, the prophet Jeremiah spiraled into a Job-like fit:

Cursed be the day when I was born;
Let the day not be blessed when my mother bore me!
Cursed be the man who brought the news
To my father saying,
"A baby boy has been born to you!"
And made him very happy.
But let that man be like the cities which the LORD overthrew
    without relenting,
And let him hear an outcry in the morning
And a shout of alarm at noon;
Because he did not kill me before birth,
So that my mother would have been my grave.
    (Jeremiah 20:14-17, NASB)

Then his groans gave way to the bleating word *why*, the Hebrew-Aramaic word *lama*:

Why [*Lama*] did I ever come forth from the womb
    To look on trouble and sorrow,
    So that my days have been spent in shame?
    (Jeremiahs 20:18, NASB)

In the same way as Job, Jeremiah became a picket who protested foot-down against God's perfect ordained plan. Pridefully, he presumed that it would've been better for him not to have been born, even though God told him at the outset of his ministry,

"Before I formed you in the womb I knew you,
And before you were born I consecrated you.
I have appointed you as a prophet to the nations. . . .
Do not be afraid of them, . . . for I am with you to deliver
    you," says the Lord.
(Jeremiah 1:4, 8, NASB).

Ungodly Anger

Job and Jeremiah became irascible. They both gave in to anger when they should not have. Granted, their agitation was sincere. It certainly was contextualized in gut-wrenching, extraordinary grief. But it was not grounded in faith. These two godly heroes lost their footing in their pain. They stumbled by denouncing their own birthdays in defiance of the sovereignty of God. Both decided God had made a mistake.

Can you imagine what it was like to be one of them? To be racked by nonstop pain and delirium. To be whirled into the throes of inner anguish. Both men of faith were so utterly disconcerted that they basically forgot who God is. They lost touch with their Creator in certain unenlightened moments. They lost touch because they clamored against the unvanquished, painful truth that God is totally trustworthy even when God allows evil to smite our lives. This is the deception of sinful anger: it belies the truth of God's faithful love.

Sinful anger lies about God's character. It forgets that God is infinitely innocent. God has no sin, no spin, no darkness, no shifting shadow, no valley of the shadow of death, and not the slightest hint of *dis*-integration. Imperfection is what causes disintegration. It disses integration. When any of us sin by being angry at God, inevitably we diss our own integrity.

The word *integrity* is related to the word *integer*, which refers to a "whole number" as opposed to a fraction. Pure integrity is wholeness. Holiness. Insofar as God is holy, there is nothing to improve. There is nothing at all in God for saintly anger to correct.

Who could ever correct the living God? Who has the omniscience to evaluate the Almighty? Who can tell the God, the potter, how to handle us, the clay?

Look at this warning in Isaiah:

"Woe to the one who quarrels with his Maker—
An earthenware vessel among the vessels of the earth!
Will the clay say to the Potter, 'What are You doing?'"
　　(Isaiah 45:9, NASB)

To be angry *with* God is to be deceived *about* God. When anger flows toward God, that anger is misguided and presumptuous. Never is it right to judge the living God. God is the judge of us (Isaiah 33:22; James 4:12).

God is good, though you and I get stung by the asp called pain. Pain is a function of Satan's fall from heaven (Luke 10:18). Pain is a consequence of sin—our sin. But pain is temporary for those of us who put our trust in Christ. Soon God will terminate our pain (2 Corinthians 4:17; Revelation 21:4). The Son of God has redeemed us from every kind of sin and all evil. Jesus has resolved the cataclysmic issue of demonic-angelic rebellion.

Though evil is still present and invasive in this world—and though everybody suffers unjustly—we nonetheless have all good things; for if we believe in Jesus, we have the Spirit of God. God gives us God's self. Thus, the only right response for you and me (and everyone) is to give ourselves reciprocally to God.

Jesus' Cry "Why?"

Jesus fully gave himself to God. He entrusted himself to no one else but God (John 2:24). I imagine part of his sorrow resided in the fact that no one else was trustworthy but God. That is not to say that Jesus was a cynic. He wasn't cynical at all. He was humble enough to know that people are fallen and self-focused, thus susceptible to deception and dishonesty. While some are prone to lying, others are inclined to being snookered. All of us, with the one exception of Jesus, tend to get confused about the truth. All of us like sheep have gone astray (Isaiah 53:6). All of us have fled from the refuge of our maker, thinking God is our enemy, not our friend. All of us have sinned by relying on our own flawed judgment.

But not Jesus. By the strength of his humility, Jesus was never deceived. Because Jesus was so humble, so truthful, so pervasively realistic, he retained his faith and gave himself to God at every point.

Look at the full extent of Jesus' humility. He was humble enough to leave heaven. Humble enough to be poor. Humble enough to be misunderstood. He was humble enough to empty himself of his divine equality with God. Jesus was even humble enough to be slapped by an insolent hypocrite who arrogantly and falsely accused him (John 18:22). He was humble enough to be hated. Humble enough to be lied to. Humble enough to be chided by his detractors as well as his students, who were quintessentially wrong in their assumptions. Jesus was humble enough to lower himself to the point of being crucified on a cross. So extraordinarily humble was Jesus. Yet his humility didn't prevent him from clearing the money changers out of the temple, or raging at the tomb of Lazarus, or railing against the Pharisees, or reproaching his disciples, or sighing in frustration at the density of people's lack of faith.

Let me say it differently: Jesus was actually humble. How many humble people have I ever really met? How many humble people do you know? Contrary to popular presumptions, humility doesn't pretend not to be talented or capable or gifted. Nor does it pretend to lack self-knowledge.

Jesus said of himself, "I am humble" (Matthew 11:29). Humility is truthful. Jesus Christ was truthful about himself. He knew who he was. His confidence was rooted in reality. Serenely, he accepted that he was a miracle worker. Never did he say, "Who am I to perform a miracle?"

Jesus had no trace of theatrical pseudo-humility. In fact, that just might explain why people didn't comment on his humility. His humility was so genuine—so utterly uncontrived—that it was simply part of his person. Thus, Jesus could simultaneously be at ease as master of all and as servant to all. So truly humble was Jesus that in his total sinlessness, he miraculously and mysteriously became sin. According to the Scriptures, God made him who knew no sin to be sin on our behalf that we might become the righteousness of God (2 Corinthians 5:21).

Jesus' sacrifice of himself was the most humble act conceivable. Though it has commonly been said that Jesus' cry of dereliction, "My God! My God! Why [*Lama*] hast Thou forsaken Me?" (Mark 15:34, NASB) was a shout of human anger, it was not. It was the greatest cry of faith in all world history. Jesus cried, "Why [*Lama*]?" precisely because his faith did *not* fail.

"My God! My God! Why [*Lama*] hast Thou forsaken Me?" That is all he said.

Jesus' cry of dereliction was not an accusation. He neither said nor insinuated that he was mad at God. Jesus did not scoff at God the Father. On the contrary, Jesus trusted God enough to retch without complaint. I don't know how to say this with enough emphasis: *It wasn't God who absorbed Jesus' wrath; it was Jesus who absorbed God's wrath.*

Notice what Jesus did *not* say. In stark contrast—in superlative contrast—to Job and Jeremiah, Jesus did not curse the day of his birth. Nor did he curse the day that the angel told Mary that she would conceive a son by the power of the Holy Spirit.

So, so far from cursing his own birthday, and so, so far from shaking a fist at God, Jesus quoted Psalm 22. That is, he spoke the first line of Psalm 22. To say the first line of a psalm is the Jewish way of referring to the psalm in its entirety. This is what Jesus was thinking as he hung naked on the cross:

My God, my God, why hast Thou forsaken me?
    Far from my deliverance are the words of my groaning.

O my God, I cry by day, but Thou dost not answer;
  And by night, but I have no rest.
Yet Thou art holy,
  O Thou who art enthroned upon the praises of Israel.
In Thee our fathers trusted;
  They trusted, and Thou didst deliver them.
To Thee they cried out, and were delivered.
  In Thee they trusted, and were not disappointed.
  (Psalm 22:1-5, NASB)

Nailed to a cross unjustly while bleeding and gasping for breath, Jesus tacitly announced that God is holy. Silently he recalled God's perfect track record. Taking refuge in the stories of the history of God's faithfulness, Jesus leaned hard into God. Humbly, he remembered the lived experience of his forefathers who waited on God and were not disappointed. Holding onto truth, Jesus trusted that he, too, would be delivered.

Yet still, Jesus' suffering persisted. Though completely overwhelmed, Jesus fixed his mind on Scripture. The Psalm continues:

But I am a worm, and not a man,
  A reproach of men, and despised by the people.
All who see me sneer at me.
They separate with the lip, they wag the head, saying,
"Commit yourself to the Lord; let Him deliver him;
Let Him rescue him, because He delights in him."
Yet Thou art He who didst bring me forth from the womb;
  Thou didst make me trust when upon my mother's
    breasts.
Upon Thee I was cast from birth;
  Thou hast been my God from my mother's womb.
  (Psalm 22:6-10, NASB)

Here again, Jesus was so far from cursing the day of his birth that he blessed it as a testimony of God's faithfulness. Jesus understood that God who delivered baby Jesus in the throes of Mary's labor would undoubtedly deliver grown-up Jesus too from the throes of torturous death. So Jesus prayed further to God:

Be not far from me, for trouble is near;
> For there is none to help.
Many bulls have surrounded me;
> Strong bulls of Bashan have encircled me.
They open wide their mouth at me,
> As a ravening and roaring lion.
I am poured out like water,
> And all my bones are out of joint.
My heart is like wax;
> It is melted within me.
My strength is dried up like a potsherd,
> And my tongue cleaves to my jaws;
> And Thou dost lay me in the dust of death.
For dogs have surrounded me;
> A band of evildoers has encompassed me;
They pierced my hands and my feet.
I can count all my bones.
They look, they stare at me.
They divide my garments among them,
> And for my clothing, they cast lots.
But Thou, O Lord, be not far off;
> O Thou, my help, hasten to my assistance.
Deliver my soul from the sword,
> My only life from the power of the dog.
Save Me from the lion's mouth

And from the horns of the wild oxen Thou dost
    answer me.
        (Psalm 22:11-21, NASB)

By faith, Jesus entered into the fullness of his pain. Jesus processed his great pain by gutting it out in truth while clinging to the truth about God. Truthfully, Jesus confessed that he was but a worm. Humbly, he admitted that he was surrounded by dogs. Yet just as truthfully, he declared that God was answering his prayer to be delivered from the horns of wild oxen. Jesus had the honesty to submit both truths: the truth that faithful God was allowing him to be trampled and the truth that Jesus' pain was not in vain.

The content of the psalm suggests that Jesus prayed in agony, not anger. I love how Jesus' prayer turned into praise:

I will tell of Thy name to my brethren;
In the midst of the assembly I will praise Thee.
You who fear the Lord, praise Him.
All you descendants of Jacob, glorify Him
And stand in awe of Him, all you descendants of Israel.
For He has not despised nor abhorred the affliction of the
    afflicted;
Neither has He hidden His face from him;
But when he cried for help, He heard.
From Thee comes my praise in the great assembly;
I shall pay my vows before those who fear Him.
The afflicted shall eat and be satisfied;
Those who seek Him will praise the Lord.
    (Psalm 22:22-26, NASB)

By faith, our crucified Lord, Jesus the bloody Lamb, concluded that God heard him in his prayer. He concluded this beforehand, in advance.

Jesus prayed this prayer while panting his last breaths. He trusted God not only for his victory over death, but also for the power of resurrection. Here's how the Psalm comes to a close:

> All the ends of the earth will remember and turn to the Lord.
> And all the families of the nations will worship before Thee.
> For the Kingdom is the Lord's,
> And He rules over the nations.
> All the prosperous of the earth will eat and worship,
> All those who go down to the dust will bow before Him,
> Even he who cannot keep his soul alive.
> Posterity will serve Him;
> It will be told of the Lord to the coming generation.
> They will come and declare His righteousness
> To a people who will be born, that He has performed it.
> (Psalm 22:27-31, NASB)

The Psalm ends boldly with a prophetic declaration of the future. God will bring it about so that "all the ends of the earth" will one day see the Lord because Jesus suffered the hardship of his unfair situation. Jesus persevered indescribable injustice by entrusting himself to God, who let the absurdity of sin run its full course. Jesus endured hostility by being humble enough to stay truthful. Jesus knew that God would reward him exponentially, because that's just how God is.

By faith, Jesus realized that even on the cross, there was no need to despair, no need at all to be anxious. Because he rested in the assurance of real faith, Jesus stayed convinced that God would soon deliver him. Indeed, faith is "the victory that overcomes the world" (1 John 5:4). On account of Jesus' faith, he was able to resist the temptation to rear up in angry pride.

What This Means for Us

What can we learn from Job, Jeremiah, and Jesus? When in pain, go to
God. Collapse on God. Turn to God. Share your agony and frustrations
with the God who hears your prayers. Bleat like a lamb—*lama . . . lama
. . . why? . . . why?*—and trust in God's deliverance, as Jesus did while
hanging on the cross.

If you find yourself angry at God, then likewise go to God, even
though God is innocent and you're not. Go straight to the living God,
as Jeremiah did. Go to God *with your anger*, instead of being like Cain,
who sublimated his anger and then pounced upon his brother with
murderous rage. Adam and Eve's son, Cain, shamefully hid his anger
from the Lord. The story of Cain's anger is found in Genesis 4. Let's look
at Genesis 4:2b-8 (NASB):

> And Abel was a keeper of flocks, but Cain was a tiller of the
> ground. So it came about in the course of time that Cain
> brought an offering to the Lord of the fruit of the ground. And
> Abel, on his part also brought of the firstlings of his flock and
> of their fat portions. And the Lord had regard for Abel and for
> his offering; but for Cain and for his offering He had no regard.
> So Cain became very angry and his countenance fell. Then the
> Lord said to Cain, "Why are you angry? And why has your
> countenance fallen? If you do well, will not your countenance
> be lifted up? And if you do not do well, sin is crouching at the
> door; and its desire is for you, but you must master it." And
> Cain told Abel his brother. And it came about when they were
> in the field, that Cain rose up against Abel his brother and
> killed him.

After God showed disregard for Cain and his faithless sacrifice,
Cain's "countenance fell" (4:6). The original Hebrew says that Cain's

"face fell." Cain literally couldn't "face" his doubt and mistrust in God. Because of Cain's unwillingness to be truthful with himself, he became unwilling to be truthful with his brother as well. Consequently, Cain could not admit that Abel's faithful sacrifice was better than his was (Hebrews 11:3).

Abel *did* trust God. That's why Cain resented him. Cain hated his brother's faith because it refracted the telling truth that Cain was not willing to face the truth. So instead of facing truth, Cain fell headlong into self-pity. See the underlying problem? Cain's face wouldn't face God's face. Therefore Cain's face fell.

Cain envied his brother Abel because Abel was content to face the truth. Abel's authenticity made it difficult for Cain to hide his own phoniness effectively. So Cain murdered Abel. In other words, Cain did *not* do what Job and Jeremiah both did—Cain did not relate to God openly and honestly with his anger. Cain failed to take his sinful anger to God. Unlike Job and Jeremiah, Cain was emotionally dishonest. Had Cain complained to God as Job and Jeremiah humbly did, I do not think Cain would have killed Abel.

When you and I are angry, we are liable to "kill Abel," so to speak, if we don't take our anger first to God. It is not irreverent to be honest with God. It's irreverent to be *dishonest* with God.

If we're already angry at God, then the best thing we can do is go to God. The only way to be restored emotionally, relationally, and spiritually is to bring our whole selves to God. When we go to God with our anger (whether we're angry at God or not), somehow God restores us. Though we fear that God might shame us, we will not be shamed. God won't take advantage of our disproportionate weakness and vulnerability. Instead, God will humbly honor our raw honesty. God "re-truths" us, if you will, when we are truthful enough to show God our complaints.

"O, Lord, all my longing is known to you," David prayed (Psalm 38:9, NRSV). God knows beforehand what we're mad about. God also knows if we're whining or if we're seriously afflicted and oppressed. God sees our flailing arms. Yet God waits for us to realize that God doesn't owe us anything; we are the ones who owe God. Still, God is so gracious. If we bring our whole selves to Jesus, God will grace us. I don't know how God does it, but God takes our selfish anger and exchanges it for joy and fills us up with mirth overflowing.

Godly Anger and Intimacy with God

I knew that my eating disorder was actually dangerous. Though I hid it skillfully, I was honest enough with myself to know that I could not keep living with such a dramatic habit. Sooner or later, it would shorten my life. I didn't want to die prematurely, so I began to face more truth.

The way I faced more truth was by meeting alone with God. I wasn't very good at it at first. I flitted in and out of my concentrated time with God alone. I would be with God for a while, reading my Bible from cover to cover, and praying prayers. Then off I'd flit again to my boyfriends and the toilet. Then I'd come back to God again. By God's grace, I'd weep sincerely at the altar. I'd confess and surrender again. Then gulp more grace.

On many, many occasions, I had breakthroughs. I peeled off layer after layer of deception. As the days and years went by, I found insight after insight. My insights were not miracles, but they were gifts from God. Little by little and leap by leap, they catapulted me forward and granted me the wisdom I needed. I can't tell you how much I learned, for instance, by writing my dissertation (this book doesn't tell it all). Studying godly anger at the level that I did—doing groundbreaking original research—lifted me to the heights of intellectual euphoria and lowered me into the bowels of my own gut-wrenching pain, where I found the greatest treasures. My pain is where I met God most intensely.

God healed me by revealing beautiful truths to replace the ugly lies that were in my head. Godly anger cleansed the temple of my mind. Though, in general, my mixed anger still violated my conscience, I became willing to hate divorce out loud in the privacy of my prayers to my creator. Instead of vomiting up food, I vomited up unrefined feelings.

All by myself, I would go to God again and not only share my thoughts, but also express to God exactly how I felt. I let go to the point that I found and felt my feelings! My unwanted negative feelings—I found them in the company of God. Just like Job and Jeremiah and King David—those pillars of faith, those fellow sinners, those spiritual mentors—I, too, experienced intimacy with God.

God touched me when I shared my most undecorated self and expressed my rawest pain. Every single time, God cheered me up. Sometimes it would take hours, but I'd stay on my knees, waiting on God in prayer, until I felt God's touch upon me again.

Cognitively, I had known God hates divorce. But I never thought to praise God for hating divorce until spontaneously I did so in the intimacy of prayer that involved my most honest emotions. The words fell out of me: "Praise God for hating divorce!"

I praised God for God's divine anger and God's high standards, even though God's holiness indicted me. The more truthful I became, the more clearly I could see that nothing can stop God from being redemptive. Yes, it was a tragedy that my parents were divorced. But God used my parents' divorce to shatter the façade of "Sweet Sarah who never got mad." God gave me eyes to see that there is no such thing as a "good Christian." Once I jettisoned the idea of trying to be a "good Christian," I found myself following Christ.

Praise God for using the very thing that crushed me (my parents' divorce) to deliver me from the deception of my persona. God freed me from my self-flattering "Christian" self-image. God ushered me out of self-righteousness, so I could see what righteousness is.

None of us are righteous (Romans 3:10). There is not even one. That's why every high-ranked Christian needs to be held accountable, just as all the rest of us do. That's why God established hell—so that we would be held accountable and not be left to our own devices. That's why every good king of Israel kept truth-telling prophets in the palace.

Apart from truth, we all drift further from God. When we aren't truthful, we aren't able to trust God. On account of our own untruthfulness, we simply cannot see how faithful God is. God is not the problem! The problem is our dishonesty about the fullness of our desperate need for Jesus.

When we finally reach the threshold of truth, the "narrow gate," as Jesus calls it (Matthew 7:13), we experience unexpected healing. I was not expecting to be healed from my eating disorder. I assumed genuine healing would never come. I thought I'd stay stuck in my bad patterns. Just as countless Christian men and women think they will always be afflicted with secret illicit behaviors, so I thought my sin habit was incurable. Praise God, I was wrong! God cured me with the healing power of anger.

Chapter 9

Can It Be Sinful *Not* to Be Angry?

In my family of origin, I was the appeaser whom everyone else could count on to be accepting and understanding and not get mad at them. I was a relational shock absorber. People could come to me in an emotionally unedited state, and usually I would be present to embrace them. On the bright side, I was warm, empathetic, and quick to laugh. But on the shadow side, I was inirascible.

The Lethargy of Inirascibility

The Bible is replete with stories of inirascible men and women—people who sinned by being angerless in their emotions. The English word *emotion* derives from the Latin root words *ex* (meaning "out") and *movere* (meaning "to move"). The word *emotion* literally means to "move out." Right emotions move people out to do the right thing. But inirascibility *keeps* people from moving out. It makes them too accepting of bad things.

Theologian Jonathan Edwards wrote in his eighteenth-century classic, *Religious Affections*, that human nature is "very lazy" unless moved by "some affection." He said, "Emotions are like springs that set us moving." He reasoned, "If all love and hatred, hope and fear, *anger* [emphasis mine] and zeal, and affectionate desire were taken away, the world would be motionless and dead." He then extrapolated this conclusion: "And if this is true of worldly affairs, it is also true in matters of faith." For Jonathan Edwards, it was evident that "the spring" of all right action unto God "lies very much in religious affections."

What an important fact for Christians to find out! Jonathan Edwards, perhaps the greatest theologian in American history, listed anger as a "religious affection." He saw anger as "religious" and as an affection that motivates right action.

Religious anger, godly anger, can motivate Christians to take right action in the midst of all the inaction that is weakening Christian ministries today. I believe epic proportions of corruption in Christian quarters are being cultivated and condoned by inirascible Christians who have a Stoic view of anger, not a Christian view of anger.

As I have already said, Stoicism is a philosophy that says anger is always wrong. It sees anger as unreasonable and useless. But Stoics have no passion for Jesus Christ. What impetus do Stoics have to clear out the temple of God? Why should a Stoic care if thieves and money changers turn a Christian organization into a business that sells anti-Christian products? What is it to a Stoic if a Christian institution self-destructs? Why be outraged if religious corporations appeal to religious defenses to hide religious corruption? What's the big deal, from a Stoic perspective, if God's name is thereby taken in vain?

Inirascible Christians have no zeal. On the contrary, they take pride in their lack of zealousness. They don't realize their inaction renders them guilty. They don't see their culpability because they're patting themselves on the back for not being angry.

Inirascibility might look like patient faith, but that is just the opposite of what it is. Inirascibility lacks the patience that it takes to stand up for what is right in the sight of God. Inirascibility is a cop-out. Biblically, we can see this in the Old Testament book of 1 Samuel in the story of Eli and his two wicked sons. Eli was a priest, and his sons, Hophni and Phineas, were priests, too. In Eli's old age, he became aware that Hophni and Phineas were defiling themselves. Both were taking precooked meat from the offering that was meant for God alone. Both were also having sexual relations in the tent meeting with women who were supposed to be serving God.

Acknowledging this corruption, Eli said to them, "Why do you do such things, the evil things that I hear from all these people? No, my sons; for the report is not good which I hear the Lord's people circulating. If one man sins against another, God will mediate for him; but if a man sins against the Lord, who can intercede for him?" (1 Samuel 2:23-24, NASB). But Eli's sons ignored him. The Bible says they "would not listen to the voice of their father" (2:25, NASB). So Eli resigned himself to his sons' sins.

What shall we make of this story? On the one hand, Eli cared enough to acknowledge that his sons had abused their power. Eli confronted them with the pained word, "Why?" He even told them that their deeds were "evil." But Eli's pain was muted. It was muffled by his inirascibility. Eli didn't care enough to be angry and consumed by the zeal of the Lord. Unlike Jesus centuries later, Eli didn't bother to cleanse the temple. So a "man of God" came to Eli with a message from the Lord that included these words: "[Thus says the LORD, (2:27, NASB)] 'Why do you kick at My sacrifice and at My offering which I commanded in My dwelling, and honor your sons above Me?' " (2:29, NASB).

According to the Scriptures, it wasn't OK with God for Eli to mellow out in his old age. Whereas Eli was content to settle for lower standards in the priesthood, God was not. God was not impressed with

Eli's casual slapping of his sons' wrists, as if accountability didn't matter. God demanded correction—restoration of integrity. God expected Eli to catalyze change. Eli had the authority to impose accountability, but Eli was emotionally too dulled.

In response, God said to him, "Those who honor me I will honor, and those who despise me shall be treated with contempt" (2:30, NASB). Soon after that episode, God removed his favor from Eli's house. Then God told the prophet Samuel, "Behold, I am about to do a thing in Israel at which both ears of everyone who hears it will tingle. In that day I will carry out against Eli all that I have spoken. . . . For I have told him that I am about to judge his house forever for the iniquity which he knew, because his sons brought a curse on themselves, and he did not rebuke them" (3:12-13, NASB).

Eli the priest committed a costly sin by *not* being angered at his sons. Yes, Eli told his sons that what they were doing was not right, but he did not rebuke them. He did not "beat back" their sacrilegious ways. Irreverently, he allowed them to abuse their authority, and in doing so, Eli himself abused his authority as well. To put it in the language of today, Eli was a bishop, so to speak, whose sin was worse than the priests' because Eli saw their guilt but covered it up.

The story of Eli shows that godly anger is a necessity at times. It also reveals that even top leaders sometimes need to be rebuked. This principle applies not only in the Old Testament, but also in the New Testament. Young Timothy, who was mentored by the apostle Paul, was directed to rebuke top Christian leaders who refused to repent from sin. In 1 Timothy 5:20, (NASB), Paul offers these instructions regarding church elders: "As for those who persist in sin, rebuke in the presence of all, so that the rest also may stand in fear."

But in Christian groups today, most people are trained to think that the elder's position serves as proof that the elder sits above accountability. Out of loyalty to the leader, we are socialized to protect the leader's position. The Bible, by contrast, teaches us to be protective of the person, not the position. In protection of the person, we are to rebuke the person. We are to "beat back" the sin that is holding that person in slavery. Because the leader is not repentant, we are also to protect the people who are being wronged under that leader's lack of leadership.

God counts it as so serious when an "elder" misuses power and instead continues in sin that God says to rebuke that "elder" in public. Not in private. Not in any face-saving, offstage venue. No, according to the God who inspired all Scripture, that unrepentant "elder" is to be rebuked "in the presence of all." In this context, I believe, the word *elder* refers to any church elder or senior pastor or denominational leader or priest or bishop or president or board chair. That is, any top spiritual leader of any Christian organization who refuses to repent should be publicly rebuked, so that the rest of the community will stay sensitive toward God, not hardened.

Why does this so rarely happen in Bible-believing communities that have unrepentant leaders who get caught? I believe the reason is that most people have not been taught that inirascibility is sinful.

The Deceptiveness of Inirascibility

Inirascible Christians forget that God judges feelings, not just actions. Thus, the prophet Jeremiah prayed, "O Lord of hosts who judges righteously, who tries the feelings and the heart" (Jeremiah 11:20, NASB). God tries our "feelings." God tests our emotions just as God tests our faith—because our emotions are *indicative* of our faith.

When I was inirascible, I valued my own sense of being popular and "in" with everyone I wanted to be "in" with. I was intentional about winning people's favor and not losing it. To me, it was anathema to have anyone displeased with me at all. So I prioritized myself, and people rewarded me for it. I was voted "favorite" and "Valentine queen." But in the deepest part of my conscience, I did not respect myself for seeking people's favor more than God's.

Self-respect requires integrity. To have integrity means to be integrated, not disintegrated; whole, not fractured. Here's how I was fractured: I had feelings I refused to engage. But what was I to do? How could I—a well-meaning Christian—possibly admit that Sweet Sarah might be angry or even have abhorrence in her heart?

That very dread is what drove my eating disorder. The deep, dark dread of pain in the form of hate drives many types of human disorders—whether a workaholic disorder, a sexual disorder, an anxiety disorder, or whatever kind of a disorder might be named. Psychological disorders including phobias and addictions often stem from unaddressed underlying pain.

No one can process pain without being honest. At the surface, of course, people can ache without being honest. We can even experience acute, unbearable pain without being honest. You can likewise exercise the defensiveness of anger—sinful anger—all you want without being honest. But you cannot process pain in the sense of working through it and getting past it unless you're brutally honest with yourself.

Jesus processed pain all the time. Jesus was a "man of suffering" (Isaiah 53:3) who prayed "with loud crying and tears" (Hebrews 5:7, NASB). That's how Jesus stayed ordered. That's how he stayed pure. Ironically, my eating disorder was not about eating and not about food. It was about my pain. It was about my anger that covered my pain. It was about my eating that dulled my anger that covered my pain.

My inirascibility caused me to stay stuck. I simply could not get well until I stopped being too high-minded, too "Christian," to be honest about my anger. I was genuinely deceived. I sublimated my feelings without consciously even realizing I had done so. I thought I had resolutely chosen to be a Christian. Christians are forbearing, right? To forbear is to bear the burden of other people's imperfection.

I thought I was being forbearing—accepting my parents' divorce for what it was.

Inirascibility deceived me. It made me think I was patient when really I was scared. It made me feel un-angry. But I was not angerless. My anger overrode me every time I starved or purged. Inirascibility tricks people. It appears to be long-suffering, but it clings for dear life to habits that suck the life right out of people. Every henpecked husband and every Stepford wife is inirascible. So is every fearful people pleaser.

Inirascibility is a sin of omission. It fails to be angry when anger is the right response. It prioritizes self without making any commotion or drawing attention to self. Inirascibility in contemporary culture is disguised as the virtue of tolerance. Indeed, tolerance is a virtue, especially in a pluralistic society, but tolerance can extend too far. I know a religious nonprofit, for instance, run by a professing Christian president who indulged in an affair with his secretary for two years with full knowledge of the Christian board. The board's inirascibility de-salted that organization.

Inirascibility puts up with diabolical activity. It pulls people into worse and worse depravity. It silences board members or prompts them to resign as soon as unsavory things begin to surface. How can a Christian board member—be it an elder or trustee—stand up against shady practices when that board member believes that truth telling is disunifying and divisive? Inirascibility tricks people into thinking it is better to be complicit than truthful.

What could be more devilish than making truthfulness appear to be a vice? "The truth hurts," it is said. "So don't be truthful. That's not loving." See the deception? The evil trick here is to make it seem unloving if anyone actually dares to be honest.

To be tolerant of dishonesty, even protective of dishonesty, is to cultivate a culture of lying. When Christian organizations foster lying instead of truth telling, people get rewarded for being

Angry Like Jesus

dishonest. Dishonesty disunifies people, but dishonesty isn't honest about that. Dishonesty flips perceptions upside down. It may *seem* to be more loving to be dishonest rather than truthful, but that is the deceitfulness of sin. One proverb puts it this way: "There is a way that seems right to a person, but its end is the way to death" (Proverbs 14:12, NASB).

When we perceive that it is better to be untruthful rather than truthful, we are bowing to the devil yet doing so in the name of bowing to God. Inirascibility doesn't really care if people bow to God or not.

The Destructiveness of Inirascibility

Inirascibility is more destructive than it might seem. Let's look at King Saul as described in 1 Samuel 15. Instead of joining in God's anger against the Amalekites, Saul befriended the Amalekite king. Despite the fact that God explicitly told Saul to destroy every tiny trace of the Amalekites' property and assets, and to utterly do away with the Amalekite people, including their king, Agag, King Saul decided instead to house King Agag and warehouse all the Amalekites' riches, including their livestock.

You see, Saul wanted glory from King Agag. I believe King Saul felt exalted by having a king subservient to him. It didn't bother Saul that King Agag and the Amelakites had disregarded God in flagrant disobedience. Saul himself, in fact, was being flagrantly disobedient to God.

King Saul was angerless, and that's what did him in. I believe his angerlessness was tied to his emptiness that made him want to fill himself with praise. King Saul thirsted to be praised. That's why he didn't care if God was praised or not. Saul's inirascibility was so offensive to God that when King Saul abused his power, God ripped Saul's kingdom away and transferred it to David instead.

Now consider King David. According to 2 Samuel 13–15, he, too, was inirascible, and his angerlessness also turned out to be disastrous. David had a heart for God, but sometimes David's sins belied his earnest love. David blew it royally as a father. He was not a good family man. He was a warrior.

When David's son, Amnon, violated David's daughter, David didn't even bother to take a stand for her. David's daughter, Tamar, was raped. Yet David was not appalled. David made no overtures to discipline Amnon or offer any nurturing to Tamar. On the contrary, David exasperated his other son, Absalom. In defense of Tamar, Absalom was outraged about what had happened to his sister. Absalom was so furious that he sabotaged his dad by leading an open rebellion, a conspiracy, a coup. So disappointed was Absalom that he literally set fire to David's fields and waged a civil war against his father. Mutiny resulted from David's sinful angerlessness. Mutiny also led to heartbreak because Absalom wound up dead.

Why didn't David care to protect his daughter? I believe past guilt immobilized and calloused David's heart. Long before Amnon ever acted on his desire to take Tamar, David had taken Bathsheba for himself (2 Samuel 11). Bathsheba was a beautiful married woman. One day when she was bathing outside on her roof, as was customary in those days, David caught a glimpse of her from afar. Little did Bathsheba know it, but David was not out fighting, though it was springtime, the season for war. Bathsheba's husband, Uriah, however, dutifully *was* fighting. David instead was hanging out in his palace, where he had no business peering out to gaze at another man's wife.

To make a long story short, David took wrong advantage of his power as Israel's king, sent someone to fetch Bathsheba for him, and managed to get her pregnant in the context of an adulterous affair. Bathsheba had no choice. David himself was in charge of the police. The king himself was the government. There was no one to rescue Bathsheba.

After David learned she was pregnant, he arranged for her husband, Uriah, to be killed on the front lines of war. In other words, lust led to adultery led to murder led to guilt. Then guilt led to inirascibility. I believe David sighed and did nothing more when Tamar was raped by Amnon because David had his own skeleton in the closet.

The subtle temptation of inirascibility originated long ago. It all began in paradise, in the Garden of Eden, as described in the book of Genesis:

> Now the serpent was more crafty than any beast of the field which the Lord God had made. And he said to the woman, "Indeed, has God said, 'You shall not eat from any tree in the garden'?" And the woman said to the serpent, "From the fruit of the trees of the garden we may eat; but from the fruit of the tree which is in the middle of the garden, God has said, 'You shall not eat from it or touch it, lest you die.'" And the serpent said to the woman, 'You shall not die! For God knows that in the day you eat from it, your eyes will be opened, and you will be like God, knowing good and evil.'" (Genesis 3:1-5, NASB)

It is no exaggeration to say "the fall" of humankind traces back to selfish angerlessness. Consider what happened. Eve was inirascible. Adam was inirascible. Neither one riled up when the serpent lied to Eve and made it sound as if God had lied to Adam. Deceitfully, the serpent framed God. That is, the serpent *misframed* God. The serpent misframed God on purpose. Yet neither Adam nor Eve was offended.

Now imagine what would have happened had Eve rebuked the serpent. What if she had said, "No way, you wily snake! Stop lying!"? That's what should have happened.

Do you remember what God told Adam and Eve? He told them to "rule" (Genesis 1:28, NASB). Explicitly they were told to rule over every living thing—including the crafty serpent—that moves upon the earth.

Men and women alike are commanded by God to subdue the earth—
and rule. We cannot, however, do that without faith. Nor can we do it
right without right anger.

The Complicity of Inirascibility

Inirascibility is passivity. It's complicity. It turns people into bystanders
who silently stand by when there's a bully. Sin is a bully. When I
kowtowed to the bully of my pride that drove my upset in the wake of
my parents' divorce, I passively stood by and did nothing. So I became
enslaved to a chronic eating disorder that promised to keep me thin and
lovable. My dad told me that no man would ever love me if I weren't
thin. With that lie at the front of my head, I clung to my eating disorder
because it gave me a sense of security that I could not find elsewhere.

I knew I was sinning with my disordered eating patterns, but I also
knew my issue was socially acceptable to others, even to Christians. It was
trendy. It was disarming. It caused people to feel superior to me—thus
comfortable and endeared to me. No one ever got mad at me for having
an eating disorder. In fact, that was another "benefit" I enjoyed. I was
able to self-destruct without facing any accountability from believers.
Isn't that tragic? Though I am thoroughly convinced that every believer
knows that anorexia and bulimia and compulsive overeating are not of
God, no one ever talked to me about the sinfulness of my sickness. Why
didn't anyone love me with right anger?

How much sooner might I have healed if Christians around me to
whom I confessed would have lovingly, inwardly raged, as Jesus did at
Lazarus's tomb? What if they would've abhorred the amnesia-causing
death of my parents' Christian marriage that led me to forget that God
is faithful? What if they would have said to me, "Sarah, we're sad *with*
you. We share anger *with* you. We are here to help you hate your parents'
divorce. We know it is a death that God hates too"?

Death swallowed up my parents' marriage. Death, the last enemy. Death, the very opposite of life. Deep within my being, I hated that enemy—that devourer. Yet I didn't know *how* to hate it. I was scared to death to hate it. Given my self-image as a Christian, I insisted upon being hate-free. In those days, I didn't see that God gives the capacity to hate and abhor because part of the Christian life is hating and abhorring sin and evil. What stood out to me back then was the nauseating stench of decaying marital flesh that issued from my parents' divorce. That constant, putrid smell made me want to empty my stomach.

I needed help from the Christian community—just as millions of other people need help from the Christian community in hating what God hates. Shared anger at hated sin can be so healing. Can you imagine how many people might be healed from their porn habits if the Christian community helped them learn to hate pornography itself, instead of just hating how they feel after they engage it? People don't engage what they actually hate. Hating porn with godly anger is a totally foreign idea to most Christians. So the norm in Christian circles is for inirascible Christians to *hide* sin together instead of hate sin together.

Inirascibility delayed my healing process. It kept me from getting well a lot sooner. It also kept me from helping others to find freedom from their self-destructive habits. Inirascibility turned me into a hider who was complicit. Way too many times, I did not call out the sins of unrepentant Christians who were sinning right in front of me—because I was unrepentant in ways as well. I didn't have godly anger against my own sins, much less theirs.

I believe complicity is one of the very biggest sins in Christianity. So many Christians relate to each other politically rather than spiritually. We swap favors. We look away. We pretend we didn't see. We wink as if corruption is no big deal. Tacitly we agree not to hold each other accountable in the name of "not being judgmental" and "being safe."

If sinning flippantly is unacceptable in the eyes of a committed Christian, that committed Christian is instantly labeled "unsafe." It used to be that safe Christians were those to whom you confess with assurance that they would guard you as they helped you to repent. But today "safe" means complicit.

Oh, that every Christian would soon become convinced that it is not safe to have "safe" friends who are inirascible! Inirascible Christians are spiritually paralyzed. They spiritually can't "move out" in godly anger. They're too tangled up and bound to help set the captives free. They can't speak up. They can't find courage. They're hampered by motivations that are ungodly. They have dark motives that don't seem dark because they're hidden in the darkness that hides behind the veneer of Christian niceness.

Many nice Christians are also inirascible in the name of "neutrality." In the sense I'm using the word, neutrality refers to avoidance rather than to the wisdom of wise boundaries. Neutrality, as I mean it, starts out as an eyewitness but then deliberately looks down for the purpose of looking away. It looks down because it knows what it already saw while looking up. To put it in biblical terms, neutrality steers clear of "the good fight of faith" (1 Timothy 6:12; 2 Timothy 4:7, NASB). It passively stands by in complicity while claiming to be ignorant of what it knows. A neutral Christian is quick to say, "I don't know anything," right after he or she learns something concrete and disenchanting that obligates that Christian to pitch in somehow and help restore just order.

God does not approve of our unwillingness to have knowledge about things we know about already. Consider what Scripture says in Proverbs 24:11-12 (New Living Translation):

> Rescue those who are unjustly sentenced to die;
>> save them as they stagger to their death.
> Don't excuse yourself by saying, "Look, we didn't know."
>> For God understands all hearts, and he sees you.

He who guards your soul knows you knew.

He will repay all people as their actions deserve.

Neutrality, as such, makes people lie. It sides with worldly power. It sees exposure of rogue power as "disrespectful." It shows loyalty to power—without regard to God's power—even as it smiles and says, "I'm neutral."

Jesus was not neutral. Neutrality is not the thing that offended the angry mob who chanted, "Crucify him!" Nowhere in the Bible is the concept of neutrality extolled. Yet it is common for professing Christians to exalt neutrality as if it were more important than loving God—or as if it were the same as loving God. Neutrality is a form of faithlessness.

Inirascibility and Rebellion

Even the nicest Christians are often faithless. The Bible says, "None are righteous, not even one." (Romans 3:10, NASB). Nice Christians have been known to scapegoat their Creator when they themselves feel jilted by God. Faithlessly, people rage against deformities, inequities, atrocities, and catastrophes that we suffer. Yet all these things are aspects of the fallenness of creation. They are not the Creator's fault. Creation didn't fall because of God. The cosmos fell due to rebellion against God. Still, human pride revolts as if the living God were the culprit. That is the insanity of sinners—we rebel against God on account of our own rebellion.

Every little trace of rebellion against God is fueled by underlying sinful anger. We all have this anger, but inirascible Christians are unwilling to admit that they have it. It's too humbling (thus feels too painful) to come to terms with. Regardless, unwanted anger is still there. Wishing it away doesn't make it disappear. It's not moisture. It does not evaporate. On the contrary, it builds up like creosote in a fireplace. If creosote in a chimney isn't regularly cleaned out, it eventually explodes.

Inirascible Christians are set up to explode, not with spewing volcanic anger, but with subterranean anger expressed in disordered behaviors such as addictions.

It's not as though angerless Christians can't see sin. Inirascibility isn't blindness. It is willfulness. It happens when Christians willfully decide to "play it safe" instead of accepting the risk of combating corruption in the midst of the Christian camp. I think of Martin Luther King Jr., who said, "Injustice anywhere is a threat to justice everywhere," except I'd like to modify his statement. What occurs to me is this: corruption anywhere in the church harms people both inside and outside the church. Many professing Christians (some of whom no longer go to church) are aware of outrageous practices happening right in front of them, but they are saying and doing nothing to halt the madness.

As long as we are inirascible Christians, we cannot help each other to experience the healing power of Jesus' anger. Jesus' anger stimulates Christians to love and do good deeds. The Greek word for "stimulate" is *paroxusmon*, which means to "stir up, irritate, provoke." God wants us to goad each other, bug each other, irritate each other into true repentance. God wants us to love and do good deeds (Hebrews 10:24).

God wants us to care about each other's spiritual progress. How many Christians believe the gospel enough to dare to stimulate another professing Christian to repent? We can't raise the standard by going along with standards that are utterly substandard to the Lord. We can't salt the earth by being neutral.

Chapter 10

Sparking a Movement of Jesus' Anger

My dad took a spiritual detour that ended up costing him his marriage with my mother. It cost everyone in our family, in fact. I was so angry about it that I contracted an eating disorder. But since I didn't know that I was angry, I simply presumed my problem was with food. Isn't that the way it happens for people with addictions and for people who suffer from symptoms that overlay their deep pain? We think the surface problem is the problem, but it's not.

It took months for me to come out of isolation and tell somebody else about my relationship with food and my obsession with having an almost-fatless body. After that, it took eight additional years for me to be unleashed from the lies that were in my head that held me down. I was so opposed to visiting my anger that I actually hid my anger from myself. Yet all along in those years, there was a big, conspicuous clue that something was off. That big clue was that I had disordered eating patterns.

So many people have problems that are clues to their underlying, unaddressed anger. The clues come in the form of sexual escapades, or drunkenness, or pilfering, or being socially absorbed in gossipy meddling, or prayerlessness, or grouchiness, or perfectionism, or legalism, or wanton shopping sprees, or any kind of control freak type of behavior. So many people are legitimately outraged about an evil in the past that their unacknowledged anger is covering up. Yet most people, including Christians, are untaught and unskilled in dealing wisely with the evil in their lives.

When I was in my twenties, I did not know how to "abhor what is evil" in a God-honoring way (Romans 12:9). So I abhorred evil in a self-destructive way. Instead of focusing my abhorrence against evil, in pride I turned my anger against myself.

Back then, I couldn't see what I had done. In my effort to be a "good Christian" who was loyal to both of my parents, I buried my honest anger—and thereby buried the honest truth of why I was so angry in the first place. Because the truth was all wrapped up inside my anger, I could not get well until I finally found the will to unearth the feelings of anger that I did not approve of in myself.

It's terrifying to dig up buried anger. Buried anger carries truth that is difficult to admit. It is scary, for example, to be honest about the hate inside our hearts. How could I, Sweet Sarah, harbor hate for my own dad? I loved my dad!

"It can't be true that I have hate for any other person; I'm just not that kind of person," I told myself. Because I thought of myself as being a true Christian, I wasn't able to be truthful with myself. Isn't that extremely ironic? There is something so pride-busting for people like me who were raised in Christian homes but not taught to be authentic at a deep emotional level. I wish I could've repented and been healed from my eating disorder a lot sooner. But instead, I launched a set of anger missiles against myself—because I hated myself for being so un-Christian.

I did not want to admit that I was angry. I wanted to be angerless and sweet. I wanted to live an anger-free life. I wanted to be neutral so that everyone would like me, including both of my parents, who no longer liked each other anymore.

But I could not manage to get myself to loosen up.

"Loosen up, Sarah, it's not that big a deal. Lots of people's parents are divorced."

Several years elapsed before it finally dawned on me that God never coldly asked me to count my parents' divorce as no big deal. It was *people* who tried to minimize what had happened. People, not God, tried to pressure me into acting as if holy matrimony isn't holy. Certain people didn't want me to be sad. They preferred that I move on and get past a tragic death that we didn't even host a funeral for. (I think there should be funerals for dead marriages.)

"Divorce happens. No grieving allowed." That is basically what I heard from people who preferred to bypass and deny the family tragedy.

But that is *not* what I heard from God. You see, God was gently present all throughout the time that I was straying from God on the one hand and seeking God on the other. In fact, the whole time I was studying godly anger—and flourishing in seminary—I was languishing with regard to my eating habits. Because for as long as I insisted on being "Sweet Sarah who never got mad," I was "Sarah who couldn't recover."

As I said before, I overcame my eating disorder by staging an intervention with myself. For nine months, no one knew about my secret. When I finally stopped quenching the Holy Spirit, I decided to reveal my secret problem to a friend I knew from church, Jim Ward.

Jim Ward attended technical school, not Baylor, where my other friends and I went. Jim Ward was not as hip or cool as the rest of us thought we were. Jim was a genuine Christian. He was the least pretentious person I knew. Jim Ward was blunt and self-deprecatory, confrontational and honest, attentive to God's word, prayerful and bighearted. I felt confident he would accept me and help me take more steps in the right direction. When I laid out the truth about my secret sin to him, he held me as I cried my makeup off.

On the day that I confessed to Jim Ward, I entered the narrow gate that Jesus said uniquely leads to life. Jesus explicitly said, "Enter by the narrow gate; for the gate is wide, and the way is broad that leads to destruction, and many are those who enter by it. For the gate is small, and the way is narrow that leads to life, and few are those who find it" (Matthew 7:13-14, NASB).

The narrow gate is small. No big, conceited head can possibly fit through it. It is a gate few people find because few are *willing* to find it. It's a doorway to the narrow path of truthfulness. I had entered that gate before, but I needed to again, because after my parents divorced, I put one foot on the broad path and kept one foot on the narrow path as well. That's what made me stuck until godly anger wrenched me out of my stuckness.

My first act of freedom was to tell on myself outright. By doing that, I rejected the status quo—my status quo. After that, I took myself to therapy. What made me do it? Holy anger against my own duplicity. I got tired of being a fake. All the compliments I got on my good figure made me feel like an imposter, since my thinness was connected to my bad secret.

So I revealed my secret. I un-secreted my secret, if you will. Once I embraced the truth about myself and about my sin—and about Christ and his love for sinners—I became able to put both of my feet on the narrow path of healing. Oh, how I love the narrow path! It is painful yet so dignifying to walk on.

Godly Anger and Pain

There's a Greek word in the original New Testament that means pain. The word is *lupe*. As in chapter 6, when I presented *embrimaomai* ("to snort like a horse") in simplified terms, I am doing the same with *lupe* here. It is not my intention to minimize the importance of technical, scholarly details. Rather, my aim is to communicate intelligibly to non-Greek readers. My goal is to display the godly anger that is there in the New Testament.

The verbal form of *lupe* is *lupeo*. Some scholars believe that *lupeo* can connote the idea of irritation or agitation. Why, then, don't our English Bibles reflect that? Given my research, I believe it is because of the Stoic influence that crept into Christianity. Evidence suggests that Bible translators gutted out the anger embedded in the Greek word *lupe* due to a long tradition of Stoic bias.

Lupe is pained anger, sorrowful anger. It is anger inside grief. Most of the time, the word *lupe* (or a form of it) is translated into English as "sorrow" or "grief" or "grieved." The English usually offers no hint of the connotation of anger that is embedded in the Greek.

It's important to acknowledge that in certain contexts, the Septuagint—the Greek translation of the Old Testament—translates Hebrew words for anger into (some form of) the Greek word *lupe*. For example, in the Septuagint in Genesis 4, Cain's murderous anger at Abel is *lupe* (*elupesen*). Cain was "very angry" (*perilupos*) when he killed Abel. Similarly, the Septuagint says that Jonah became angry (*lupev*) because he was so displeased (*elupethe*) with God's decision to relent from bringing calamity upon the city of Nineveh (Jonah 4:1).

Bearing this in mind, let's review a few occurrences of *lupe* in the New Testament.

The Ruler's *Lupe*

All three Synoptic Gospels (Matthew, Mark, and Luke) tell the story of the ruler who walked away from Jesus. The New American Standard Bible renders Luke's account to read like this:

A certain ruler questioned Him [Jesus], saying, "What shall I do to inherit eternal life?"

Jesus answered, "You know the commandments: Do not commit adultery; do not murder; do not steal; do not bear false witness; honor your father and mother."

The ruler replied, "All these things I have kept from youth."

So Jesus said to him, "One thing you still lack: Sell all that you possess and distribute it to the poor, and you shall have treasure in heaven, and come, follow Me" (Luke 18:18-22).

Traditionally, English Bible translators have said that when the ruler heard Jesus' answer, he became "very sad." Let's pause to think about this, because it really doesn't make much sense. If the ruler was purely sad and nothing more, then why didn't he linger longer to ask Jesus to find a way to allow him keep his money *and* follow Jesus? The ruler conceivably could have said, "But Jesus, I'll fund your ministry," or something to that effect. But he did not. Instead, the rich young ruler walked away.

I believe he left in a muted huff. The Gospel of Luke says the ruler became *perilupos*. The Greek word *perilupos*, as we already know, is the very same word that the Septuagint uses to describe the selfish anger of Cain (Genesis 4:6). The gospel writer Matthew says this ruler was "young" and "owned much property" (Matthew 19:22). The gospel writer Mark says that when the ruler heard Jesus' reply, the ruler's "face fell." His face fell just as Cain's face fell. In Greek, the phrase is this: *ho de stugnasas.* The verb is from *stugnos*, which here means "shocked" or "appalled."

To put it plainly, the rich young ruler was appalled at Jesus' answer. How dare Jesus speak like that to a ruler! Especially to a ruler who had such a good track record! How galling it was for this ruler to be told in such clear terms that he needed to give his riches to the poor! How insulting it was to be told that the price of eternal life was to give up all he had and follow Jesus!

The rich young ruler wasn't interested in Jesus. He was interested in immortality. How common is it for the very most privileged people to want to extend themselves by memorializing themselves? Almost every wealthy ruler wants to be eternalized and remembered by all posterity.

Jesus understood that the rich young ruler wasn't truly interested in life. The ruler was pursuing an extension of himself without God. You see, the ruler loved his money, not God. Love of money keeps many (both rich and poor) from entering the kingdom of God. Love of money entangles people in the matrix of serving mammon, a false god. Since mammon itself is false, those who worship it turn into phonies. Mammon produces imposters. Imposters, by definition, are deceivers. Deceivers are people who lie. Mammon makes people lie as this ruler lied to Jesus about having obeyed the commandments in full.

As a result of his encounter with Jesus, I believe, this ruler realized deep down inside that Jesus knew he had lied. So the ruler hardened himself—because that's what liars do. They harden themselves with each successive lie.

Jesus was exposing this young ruler. Jesus drew out the fact that the rich young ruler lived in constant violation of the first of the Ten Commandments, which is to have no other gods before God. This ruler bowed to money. He was enslaved to his own money. This ruler was not a ruler when it came to the ruler's wealth. Nor was he a ruler with regard to his foreboding mortality.

Yes, the rich young ruler came to Jesus. But he did not want Jesus. He walked away from Jesus knowingly. The ruler clearly knew that Jesus holds the keys to eternal life. It's not explicit in the text, but I believe this ruler wanted access to the keys, so to speak. The ruler wanted power, more and more power, even the power to extend to his power into eternity.

I believe that mammon deceived this ruler into thinking that power and money are holier than God. That's the lie that turned this ruler into a liar. As I explained in chapter 4, liars are so deceived that they prefer hell over heaven. Now we see this ruler who rejected Jesus' love (Mark 10:21). The text implies that this ruler did not want Jesus' love. Because this ruler rejected truth—by bowing to the false god mammon—this ruler became "very angry" (*perilupos*) with sinful anger when Jesus exposed the truth that this ruler valued power over love.

King Herod's *Lupe*

King Herod is famous for having chopped off John the Baptist's head. That gruesome murder happened because John the Baptist boldly told King Herod that Herod's incestuous marriage to Herod's brother's wife, Herodias, was unlawful. To say it more accurately, it wasn't King Herod who went after John the Baptist. It was Herodias.

After Herodias found out what John had said about her marriage, she desired for John to be obliterated. But Herodias had found no way, legitimately, to eliminate John (Mark 6:18-19). Had her husband, King Herod, shared her same bloodthirstiness for John the Baptist's head, Herodias easily could have had John the Baptist sent to the gallows without cause. But since King Herod delighted in John, and even *feared* John a bit, given that he could see that John was a righteous man (6:20), Herod chose merely to bind John and arrest him (6:17).

While John was in confinement, he was just fine until the strategic day that King Herod threw a party for himself. Because it was Herod's birthday, he hosted an elaborate banquet before "his lords and military commanders and the leading men of Galilee" (6:21). All these lofty men were present in the room when the daughter of Herodias came in to dance for Herod and his guests. To say the least, the men were pleased with her.

So the king said to the girl, right there in public, "Ask me for whatever you want, and I will give it to you" (6:22). He actually swore to her, "Whatever you ask of me, I will give it to you, up to half of my kingdom" (6:23, NASB).

The girl went out and asked her mother what to request. Herodias told her plainly, "The head of John the Baptist" (6:24). So Herodias's daughter rushed back and said to Herod in front of his guests, "I want you to give me right away the head of John the Baptist on a platter" (6:25).

How did King Herod respond to this emotionally? The Bible says he had *lupe* (*lupetheis*). Granted, Herod's *lupe* probably had real sadness in it for John. Still, I believe Herod's *lupe* was mostly charged with anger against his crafty wife who outmaneuvered him by trapping him with his own inflated ego.

The Slaves' *Lupe* in a Story Jesus Told

In Matthew 18:21-34, Jesus tells about a king who wished to settle his accounts. As the story goes, there was brought to this king a slave who owed the king ten thousand talents (the equivalent of at least $10 million) but was unable to repay. So the king commanded him to be sold, along with his wife and children and all that he had, so that the slave could settle his bill. But the slave dropped down and prostrated himself and pled before the king, saying, "Have patience with me, and I will pay you everything" (18:26, NASB).

In response, the king felt compassion for him and released him and forgave his debt. That forgiven slave, however, went out with a double standard and found one of his fellow slaves who owed him a mere hundred denarii (the equivalent of three months' worth of slave wages), and seized him and began to choke him, saying, "Pay what you owe!" (18:28).

The fellow slave fell down and began to entreat him, saying, "Have patience with me, and I will pay you" (18:29). But the forgiven slave was unwilling to extend the same mercy that he himself had been given in far, far greater abundance by the king. So ruthless was this ungrateful forgiven slave that he threw the lower slave into prison.

When some other fellow slaves saw what had happened, they had a form of *lupe* (*elupethesin*). Did their *lupe* comprise mere sadness? No doubt, they felt sad to see their fellow worker so mistreated. Still, I believe they were angry. They had a lot to be angry about: their fellow slave had physically been seized and choked, even imprisoned and attacked for not yet paying back a debt that amounted to a small fraction of what his creditor had undeservedly been forgiven of. The fellow slaves were outraged—angered—by the cruelty and hypocrisy of the forgiven nonforgiver who refused to pass down the grace shown to him.

When the king found out what the nonforgiver had done, he summoned him and said, "You wicked slave, I forgave you all that debt because you pleaded with me. Shouldn't you have had mercy on your fellow slave, as I had mercy on you?" (18:31-33). Then the king handed him over to the torturers.

There is a lot to discuss in this story, given that it speaks of anger and slaves and torturers. Rather than develop such a discussion, I will simply say that both slavery and torture are extreme violations of the Golden Rule: "You shall love your neighbor as yourself" (Matthew 22:39). A big part of loving our neighbor is abhorring any "evil" that invades them (Romans 12:9).

The Holy Spirit's *Lupe*

Even the Spirit of God experiences *lupe*. In Ephesians 4:30, we are all commanded not to *lupeite* the Holy Spirit of God. We are not to grieve God as the disciples grieved Jesus when they didn't choose to put their trust in him. I believe God is grieved with anger-filled sadness when Christians fail to "put away our former life, your old self, corrupt, and deluded by its lusts" (Ephesians 4:22).

Yet I must confess: I don't know what it means for God to be grieved. Does it mean that God shuns our prayers? Does God withhold grace from us or remove angelic protection? Does God afflict us? I don't think it is wise to frame questions in this way, because the questions I have just posed are all focused on self-interest. When we ask merely about own sense of good welfare, we are thinking about ourselves, not God.

The question, though, is important: What does it mean to grieve the Holy Spirit? Allow me to answer from this angle. The Bible calls God's Spirit the "Spirit of truth" (John 14:17; 16:13, NASB). The Spirit is grieved when people rebel against the Spirit of Truth. Resisting truth, hiding truth, covering up truth by replacing it with lies—these are ways to directly grieve God's Spirit.

I believe God is angered, not just saddened, by deceivers—especially by willful deceivers who pretend to be believers. To do evil in God's name is to take God's name in vain. As the *New Revised Standard Version puts it, to make a "wrongful use" of God's name is to break the Third Commandment (Exodus 20:7)*. Caution: This is the only commandment among the Ten Commandments that comes with a built-in judgment. Here's the full text of the Third Commandment: "You shall not make wrongful use of the name of the Lord your God, for the Lord will not acquit anyone who misuses his name." So you see, the judgment is that God will "not acquit anyone" who uses God's holy name to overpower the weak or hide truth.

Godly *Lupe*

It is explicit in the Scriptures that sometimes *lupe* is godly. The apostle Paul writes about "godly" *lupe* (*theon lupe*) in 2 Corinthians 7:8-11 (NASB):

For though I caused you [*lupe*] by my letter, I do not regret it; though I did regret it—for I see that that letter caused you [*lupe*], though only for a little while—I now rejoice, not that you were made [*lupe*], but that you were made [*lupe*] to the point of repentance; for you were made [*lupe*] according to the will of God, in order that you might not suffer loss in anything through us. For the [*lupe*] that is according to the will of God produces a repentance without regret, leading to salvation; but the [*lupe*] of the world produces death. For behold what earnestness this very thing, this **godly [*lupe*]** has produced in you; what vindication of yourselves, what indignation, what fear, what longing, what zeal, what avenging of wrong!

Most English versions of Scripture translate the Greek word *lupe* here as "sorrow." But the passage makes far more sense if the word *lupe* is understood to mean "pained anger." Consider the cluster of concepts that Paul addresses here: vindication, indignation, fear (i.e., reverence), longing, zeal, avenging of wrong.

The whole passage becomes eye-opening when we read it as a teaching on the virtue of godly anger:

> For though I caused you **anger** by my letter, I do not regret it; though I did regret it—for I see that that letter caused you **anger**, though only for a little while—I now rejoice, not that you were made **angry**, but that you were made **angry** to the point of repentance; for you were made **angry** according to the will of God, in order that you might not suffer loss in anything through us. For the **anger** that is according to the will of God produces a repentance without regret, leading to salvation; but the **anger** of the world produces death. For behold what earnestness this very thing, this **godly anger** has produced in you; what vindication of yourselves, what indignation, what fear, what longing, what zeal, what avenging of wrong!

Godly anger motivates people to repent. It accords "with the will of God" (2 Corinthians 7:9-10) because it moves us to "abhor what is evil" and "cling to what is good" (Romans 12:9, NASB). Godly anger leads repenters to salvation (2 Corinthian 7:10)!

By contrast, the anger (*lupe*) of the world produces death. Worldly anger caused the homicide of Cain's younger brother, Abel. Worldly anger tried to annihilate the Jews. Worldly anger strategized to decapitate John the Baptist. Let us be warned: it is the nature of worldly anger to produce dark motivations that cause people to be selfish enough to kill, steal, and destroy.

The paradox is this: godly anger unseats sinful anger. Godly anger is so good that it battles against the evil of worldly anger. Godly anger is holy discontent. It turns people into Popeye, the cartoon sailor man who in every TV episode intervenes with godly anger. Popeye fights against evil and shouts with endearing resolve, "That's all I can stands; I can't stands no more!"

Godly anger is heroic. It subverts the power of evil by championing the truth.

A Global Movement of Godly Anger

Godly anger fights the good fight of faith (1 Timothy 6:12). It does not go to war for the ideology of an ism. It is not driven, for example, by abstract conceptual notions such as socialism or communism or capitalism or Catholicism or evangelicalism or feminism or environmentalism or pacifism. All these isms become idols. Godly anger is not idolatrous. It is worshipful toward God, who divinely loves all people whom these isms try so desperately to protect.

Godly anger fights against evil. Why does God allow evil in this world? That is not the best question I can think of. A better question is this: How can *you and I allow evil that we see* to grow and fester in local churches and Christian nonprofits and in each other and our own hearts? If the church is not salted with godly anger, truth, and love, how then can the world be salted? Jesus said that "you" are the salt of the earth (Matthew 5:13). The world needs *you* to be salt—to be an irritant, a preserver, a healer.

The world will be more healed when you and I become more healed. We, as Christians, *can* be healed. But not without each other's help. I need you to be salt. I need you to irritate me in a godly way. Please prod me to repent. Please set a good example. Inspire me. Help preserve me. Please give me your best input. Tell me the truth. Don't burden me with fake Christian niceness. Instead, love me lavishly with a generous desire to see me soar. Talk to me in person. Sit down with me and face me. Sing psalms and hymns to me, and pray for God to change me. Get the log out of your eye, so that you can remove the speck from my eye (Matthew 7:1-5).

I need you to become "logless," so that I can become "speckless." I cannot get the speck out of my own eye. I can only remove the log. I want to be speckless. I want to see clearly, so I will see more truth—and thereby trust God more. I long to trust God more, so I will obey God more, and know God more, and love God more. The more I love God, the bigger capacity I will have to love you. The more I love you, the more you will be loved. The more you are loved, the more you can be healed. See how the cycle works?

Start the cycle. I'll start the cycle, too. Let's get healed. Let's salt the earth. If you're mad at me for having sinned against you, please let me know, so I can tell you how sorry I am and pray for you and do my part to restore you. Likewise, if you're envious of me, thinking I have it made and you don't, please confess it. I want to be your cheerleader. I want to help you know how neat it is to be you!

If you're mad at yourself, then please confess that too. God can give you godly anger to hate your unforgiveness and harshness toward yourself. You *can* learn to hate your own rejection of God's grace. You *can* absorb God's love.

What I'm saying is hope abounds. There is hope! There is hope for you, and there is hope for me. Long ago, I wrote a song about this.

When I sing it, people tend to cheer up. It's a simple little ditty, and it goes like this:

> There is hope, for even me.
> There is hope, for even me.
> It blows my mind.
> All of the time.
> But there's still hope, for even me.

The second verse is to be sung from one person to another, smile to smile, and eye to eye:

> There is hope, for even you.
> There is hope, for even you.
> It blows your mind.
> All of the time.
> But there's still hope, for even you.

No matter what you've done, there is hope for you if you will just be honest. Tell yourself the truth. Get real with yourself again in a brand-new way. Set every excuse aside. Tell yourself fully the unedited version of what you feel deprived of. Tell *God* what you feel deprived of. Tell God what you don't like about your life. Tell God what you don't like about yourself. Tell God what someone did that hurt your feelings. Tell God all about it. Pour out your heart to God.

Share with God how you feel about what has happened to you in your life. Take time to be with God in the most intimate, honest way unhurriedly. Don't worry about anyone hearing you or judging you. None of us are the judge. Only God is the judge. God already knows about you anyway, so you might as well open up to God in private. God will be there when you cough up your deep pain. God longs to be gracious to you. God has the power to re-grace you, so that you won't feel afraid or dirty or defective anymore. God can re-salt you, so you will be salted enough to help the larger Christian community get re-salted.

We cannot salt the earth if we are winking at misconduct in the ranks of Christianity. Christian winking makes a mockery of the gospel. Yet how many Christians are winking by choosing "loyalty" and "unity" and "neutrality"? It is *not* loyal to Jesus to choose loyalty over integrity and love. Nor is it unifying for Christians to unite in shallow niceness. Nor is it neutral to stay silent about corruption taking place in Christian endeavors.

Anecdotally, I know way too many stories of political cover-ups in Christian churches and organizations and Christian schools. I bet readers of this book know stories, too, that should not be. What are we going to do? What are *you* going to do?

I vote this: let's inspire our non-Christian friends by showing them what biblical Christian love looks like from Christian to Christian. Let's become an illustration of what happens when we repent from unforgiveness and bitter jealousy and self-hatred. Let's show our non-Christian friends the marvel of what happens when we forgive and root for each other and do everything we can to help each other improve and excel. Let's hold each other accountable instead of shrugging in helplessness as if we are not salted enough to salt each other.

Let's bow down on our knees and humbly ask God to grace us with blessed *lupe*—blessed anger—that can catapult us out of the status quo.

Godly Anger and Healing

People tell me I "have guts." Well, the reason I have guts is that Jesus *healed* my gut. I'm like Mary Magdalene, who was healed from seven demons. I have sweet firsthand experience of being touched inside by God. God touched me, not in my guardedness but in my vulnerability. Vulnerability is a prerequisite for healing. I decided to be vulnerable at an honest emotional level with God and also with others, and that has made all the difference. I have *lived* the sermon I am preaching. I am walking proof that godly anger has power to heal.

Godly anger holds the power to bring healing to you, too—you're healable. Don't discount what God can do for you. You just need the vulnerability of truth. Be truthful. Don't kid yourself. Find the "Jim Ward" in your community. Go tell an honest person what you honestly did wrong. And if you haven't done so already, let someone know your story, because somewhere in your story, you were wronged. It's not your fault that you were hit by someone else's evildoing.

Godly anger helps people make peace with the truth. It exposes deeds of darkness. It repents from hypocrisy. It refuses bitterness and isolation. It kicks the habit, and tells the truth, and collapses in surrender unto God. It takes solidarity with Jesus. It generates moral courage and moral leadership.

Biblically, we see that godly anger rescues babies, even when the government says to kill them (Exodus 1:15-17). It meets with Egypt's Pharaoh and says, "Let God's people go!" (Exodus 8:1). It runs swiftly toward Goliath with a bag of five smooth stones (1 Samuel 17:48-49). It spotlights Haman's underlying treachery (Esther 7:6). It rebuilds Jerusalem's wall in fifty-two days (Nehemiah 6:15). It notifies King Herod—boldly face-to-face—that his marriage is unlawful (Luke 3:19). It publicly reproves the apostle Peter (Galatians 2:12-14).

"Not by might, not by power, but by My Spirit," says the Lord (Zephaniah 4:4, NASB). Godly anger gets it—that the battle is the Lord's. So godly anger fights with prayer and perseverance and love that makes it stronger even than death.

Godly anger says no to shady practices. It offers a holy no. Not a "hell, no" but a holy no that refuses to cooperate with lies and covered up lies and covered-up truth. Godly anger chooses truth. It chooses Jesus.

The same Jesus who cleared the temple has risen from the dead, and now his head is "white like wool, like snow, and his eyes are like a flame of fire, and his feet are like burnished bronze when it has been caused to glow in a furnace, and his voice is like the sound of many waters" (Revelation 1:14-15, NASB). When the apostle John saw *this* Jesus, he collapsed at Jesus' feet like a dead man.

John says Jesus' face was shining like the sun (Revelation 1:16). Most people can barely tolerate the intensity of being looked at by someone who is peering into their person. Most people look away if someone tries to engage them eye to eye with radiant truthfulness and love. I contend that Jesus saw right through the apostle John, and that John felt it, so he collapsed.

It didn't matter that John had been chosen to be in Jesus' inner circle as an apostle. John's soul was stripped and naked. John was completely laid bare. No excuse could cover him. John, the sinner, I believe, was completely found out, fully exposed. So John fell as a dead man. Like Isaiah, he understood that he was "ruined" (Isaiah 6:5).

Then Jesus put his hand on John.

As I envision John's vision, the apostle John experienced terrorizing exposure followed by the most powerful gentle touch that had ever alighted on him. John felt Jesus spiritually touching the deepest part of him that Jesus had, just prior to that, exposed.

Then the waters of Jesus' voice became so soothing. Like the sloshing gentle sound of running water through a stream, so Jesus' voice comforted him. "Do not be afraid," said Jesus (Revelation 1:17).

The risen Lord, who loves you—who shed his blood for you—is telling you today, "Do not be afraid." Stand for what is right. God has your back. If you will patiently be still and ask God's Spirit to help you sense where Jesus' hand of protection is physically on your back, you just might sense it. You might then become convinced that you're not "out there" on your own. If you entrust yourself to Christ, you'll be OK.

I believe it's time for a critical mass of Christians to decide to live out our calling as Christ followers. It's time to get right on mission by acting more like Christians who fight on behalf of others with otherworldly weapons of truth and honest faith and genuine love. Jesus guarantees us we won't lose. He promised to build his church. He said, "The gates of hell will not prevail against it" (Matthew 16:18, NASB).

Jesus stormed the gates of hell by making disciples. He poured forgiveness into people and infused their imaginations with truthful revelations about God. He ate with tax gatherers and harlots (Matthew 9:11). He preached and fed and healed and felt compassion for the multitudes. He regarded Mary and Martha as his protégés (Luke 10:39-42). He called fishermen and lawyers to himself. He spent hours in the night mentoring Nicodemus, a powerful ruler who felt afraid to come to Jesus during the day (John 3:1-21). Jesus risked his life to turn a demoniac into a messenger of God (Luke 8:22-39). He told the city of Jerusalem that he longed to gather her people "as a hen gathers her brood under her wings" (Luke 13:34, NASB). Jesus welcomed children to disciple-making parties because we are all invited to serve God.

It's time to worship God, even for God's wrath. It's time to imitate Jesus, even in his ever-loving anger. It's time to take out matches to light the fire of revival in local churches and Christian schools and organizations. Godly anger can spark a movement of moral courage that gives us confidence to repent from being lazy and complacent. Godly anger can stoke our hearts with the fire of heavenly love that stirs us to love each other as ourselves.

Movements happen when people start moving. So let's get moving. Let's do *something* rather than nothing. Let's care enough to dare to raise the standard.

Closing Prayer

There's an old Franciscan prayer that I am personally praying for every reader of this book:

> May God bless you with discomfort at easy answers,
> half-truths, and superficial relationships,
> so that you may live deep within your heart.
>
> May God bless you with anger at injustice,
> oppression and exploitation of people, so that
> you may work for justice, freedom and peace.
>
> May God bless you with tears to shed for those who
> suffer from pain, rejection, starvation, and war, so that
> you may reach out your hand to comfort them
> and turn their pain to joy.
>
> And may God bless you
> with enough foolishness [that the Bible calls "faith"]
> to believe that you can make a difference in this world,
> so that you can do what others claim cannot be done.
>
> Amen.

I believe this prayer from www.aheartforjustice.com is part of the public domain.

About the Author

Dr. Sarah Sumner is a change agent. She is the first woman to graduate with a Ph.D. in Systematic Theology from Trinity Evangelical Divinity School in Deerfield, Illinois. She is the only woman in the United States to have been Dean and Full Professor of a conservative evangelical seminary. After only sixteen months under her leadership, A. W. Tozer Theological Seminary broke two consecutive records for all-time high enrollment in the thirty-four-year history of the school. The seminary also ended financially in the black for the first time ever.

Dr. Sumner has a unifying vision of how to mobilize genuine Christians, so that we stand with moral courage and speak the truth in love, even in the face of opposition. She is the founder of Right On Mission, a movement-based, movement-building business that offers consulting services and mission statement services globally to believers around the world. If you haven't made an appointment yet to get Sarah or one of her colleagues to write a mission statement that motivates you personally or sparks your local church or rejuvenates your Christian organization, just google www.rightonmission.org.

Dr. Sumner is Founding President of Right On Mission ACADEMY, a cutting-edge, quasi-online "vocational seminary" recently established in 2015 that offers college-level and graduate-level programs that students can fund themselves without tapping into government student loans. The mission of the Academy is "to teach students to think so Christianly that they find the moral courage to act with integrity as Christ followers." See www.rightonmissionacademy.org.

Sarah is gladly married to Jim Sumner, her dance partner, life partner, and partner in forgiveness.

She has written three other books:

Men and Women in the Church: Building Consensus on Christian Leadership (2003)
Leadership above the Line (2006)
Just How Married Do You Want to Be? (2008)